FODOR'S BERMUDA 2006
Editor: Jacinta O'Halloran

Editorial Production: David Downing
Editorial Contributors: Robyn Bardgett, Liz Jones, Dale Leatherman, Terri Mello, Catalina Stovell, Sarah Titterton, James Whittaker, Carla Zuill
Maps: David Lindroth, *cartographer;* Rebecca Baer and Bob Blake, *map editors*
Design: Fabrizio La Rocca, *creative director;* Guido Caroti, *art director;* Melanie Marin, *senior picture editor*
Production/Manufacturing: Colleen Ziemba
Cover Photo: Bill Bachmann/Positive Images

SPECIAL SALES
This book is available for special discounts for bulk purchases for sales promotions or premiums. Special editions, including personalized covers, excerpts of existing books, and corporate imprints, can be created in large quantities for special needs. For more information, write to Special Markets/ Premium Sales, 1745 Broadway, MD 6-2, New York, New York 10019, or e-mail specialmarkets@ randomhouse.com.

AN IMPORTANT TIP & AN INVITATION
Although all prices, opening times, and other details in this book are based on information supplied to us at press time, changes occur all the time in the travel world, and Fodor's cannot accept responsibility for facts that become outdated or for inadvertent errors or omissions. So **always confirm information when it matters,** especially if you're making a detour to visit a specific place. Your experiences—positive and negative—matter to us. If we have missed or misstated something, **please write to us.** We follow up on all suggestions. Contact the Bermuda editor at editors@fodors.com or c/o Fodor's at 1745 Broadway, New York, NY 10019.

PRINTED IN THE UNITED STATES OF AMERICA

10 9 8 7 6 5 4 3 2 1

Be a Fodor's Correspondent

Your opinion matters. It matters to us. It matters to your fellow Fodor's travelers, too. And we'd like to hear it. In fact, we *need* to hear it.

When you share your experiences and opinions, you become an active member of the Fodor's community. That means we'll not only use your feedback to make our books better, but we'll publish your names and comments whenever possible. Throughout our guides, look for "Word of Mouth," excerpts of your unvarnished feedback.

Here's how you can help improve Fodor's for all of us.

Tell us when we're right. We rely on local writers to give you an insider's perspective. But our writers and staff editors—who are the best in the business—depend on you. Your positive feedback is a vote to renew our recommendations for the next edition.

Tell us when we're wrong. We're proud that we update most of our guides every year. But we're not perfect. Things change. Hotels cut services. Museums change hours. Charming cafés lose charm. If our writer didn't quite capture the essence of a place, tell us how you'd do it differently. If any of our descriptions are inaccurate or inadequate, we'll incorporate your changes in the next edition and will correct factual errors at fodors.com *immediately.*

Tell us what to include. You probably have had fantastic travel experiences that aren't yet in Fodor's. Why not share them with a community of like-minded travelers? Maybe you chanced upon a beach or bistro or B&B that you don't want to keep to yourself. Tell us why we should include it. And share your discoveries and experiences with everyone directly at fodors.com. Your input may lead us to add a new listing or highlight a place we cover with a "Highly Recommended" star or with our highest rating, "Fodor's Choice."

Give us your opinion instantly at our feedback center at www.fodors.com/feedback. You may also e-mail editors@fodors.com with the subject line "Bermuda Editor." Or send your nominations, comments, and complaints by mail to Bermuda Editor, Fodor's, 1745 Broadway, New York, NY 10019.

You and travelers like you are the heart of the Fodor's community. Make our community richer by sharing your experiences. Be a Fodor's correspondent.

Happy traveling!

Tim Jarrell, Publisher

CONTENTS

CLOSEUPS

ABOUT THIS BOOK

Our Ratings

Sometimes you find terrific travel experiences and sometimes they just find you. But usually the burden is on you to select the right combination of experiences. That's where our ratings come in.

As travelers we've all discovered a place so wonderful that its worthiness is obvious. And sometimes that place is so experiential that superlatives don't do it justice: you just have to be there to know. These sights, properties, and experiences get our highest rating, Fodor's Choice, indicated by orange stars throughout this book.

Black stars highlight sights and properties we deem Highly Recommended, places that our writers, editors, and readers praise again and again for consistency and excellence.

By default, there's another category: Any place we include in this book is by definition worth your time, unless we say otherwise. And we will.

Disagree with any of our choices? Care to nominate a place or suggest that we rate one more highly? Visit our feedback center at www.fodors.com/feedback.

Budget Well

Hotel and restaurant price categories from ¢ to $$$$ are defined in the opening pages of each chapter. For attractions, we always give standard adult admission fees; reductions are usually available for children, students, and senior citizens. Want to pay with plastic? AE, D, DC, MC, V following restaurant and hotel listings indicate if American Express, Discover, Diner's Club, MasterCard, and Visa are accepted.

Restaurants

Unless we state otherwise, restaurants are open for lunch and dinner daily. We mention dress only when there's a specific requirement and reservations only when they're essential or not accepted—it's always best to book ahead.

Hotels

Hotels have private bath, phone, TV, and air-conditioning and operate on the European Plan (a.k.a. EP, meaning without meals), unless we specify that they use the Continental Plan (CP, with a continental breakfast), Breakfast Plan (BP, with a full breakfast), or Modified American Plan (MAP, with breakfast and dinner) or are all-inclusive (including all meals and most activities). We always

list facilities but not whether you'll be charged an extra fee to use them, so when pricing accommodations, find out what's included.

Many Listings

★	Fodor's Choice
★	Highly recommended
✉	Physical address
✛	Directions
⌂	Mailing address
☎	Telephone
🖷	Fax
⊕	On the Web
✆	E-mail
💷	Admission fee
☉	Open/closed times
►	Start of walk/itinerary
▭	Credit cards

Hotels & Restaurants

🏨	Hotel
🛏	Number of rooms
♿	Facilities
❞◎❝	Meal plans
✕	Restaurant
☞	Reservations
🎩	Dress code
✎	Smoking
⊕❞	BYOB
✕🏨	Hotel with restaurant that warrants a visit

Outdoors

🏌	Golf
⛺	Camping

Other

☺	Family-friendly
🖪	Contact information
⇨	See also
✉	Branch address
☞	Take note

BERMUDA'S PARISHES	
	When the 1610 Bermuda Company divided up the islands of Bermuda among its seven original shareholders, Bermuda's parishes, or districts, were delineated into shares (25 acres per share) and tribes (50 shares per tribe). The nine parishes are named after these early Bermuda Company investors—Sandys, Southampton, Warwick, Paget, Pembroke, Devonshire, Smith's, Hamilton, and St. George's—who were, as in "Humpty Dumpty," all the king's men: aristocrats, knights, some members of parliament, who financed or played a role in Bermuda's colonization. Though parish boundaries no longer delineate property ownership, they now function as the small island version of state or province lines. Bermudian's are parochially proud and whether from the *West End* (anything west of the city of Hamilton), the *East End* (anything east of the city of Hamilton), or the *Town* (the city of Hamilton and its surrounding parishes), allegiances are quite publicly paraded when Cup Match—the annual cricket festival where East faces West—rolls around in July.
HAMILTON	
	Despite its name, Hamilton Parish has nothing to do with the city of the same name. The city of Hamilton is in Pembroke Parish; Hamilton Parish is west of St. George's. Home to many of Bermuda's wealthiest residents, bustling Hamilton Parish is a very walkable parish with lots to see, and it makes for a full day's sightseeing—no need to stay here. Must-sees include the Crystal Caves, Bailey's Bay, Bermuda Aquarium, the North Shore Road, Bermuda Railway Museum, Tom Moore's Jungle, and the Bermuda Perfumery and Gardens.
SMITH'S	
	Historical Flatts Village, crowded along the edge of one of the most beautiful and quaint harbors in Bermuda, is the de facto center of Smith's Parish, which borders Harrington Sound and is home to the Devil's Hole Aquarium, Spittal Pond nature reserve, Spanish Rock, and Verdmont Historic House, an 18th century estate. There are plenty of historic and natural attractions, good beaches, and good places to stay, but you'll have to travel to the other parishes for dining and nightlife options.

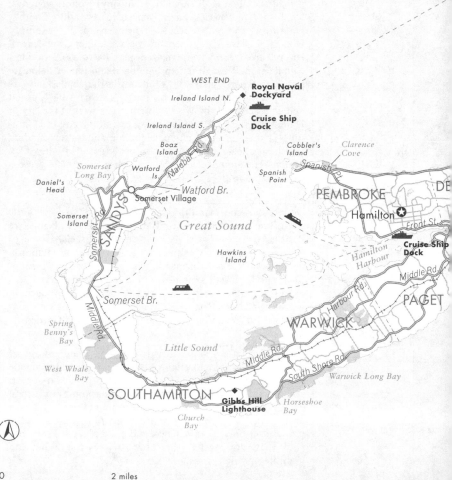

Bermuda

KEY
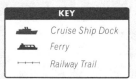
🚢 *Cruise Ship Dock*
⛴ *Ferry*
⊢——⊣ *Railway Trail*

WEST END

Royal Naval
Dockyard

Ireland Island N.

**Cruise Ship
Dock**

Ireland Island S.

Cobbler's
Island

Clarence
Cove

Boaz
Island

Spanish Pt.

Somerset
Long Bay

Watford
Is.

Spanish
Point

PEMBROKE

Daniel's
Head

Watford Br.

Hamilton

Somerset Village

SANDYS

Great Sound

Somerset
Island

Front St.

**Cruise Ship
Dock**

Hawkins
Island

Hamilton
Harbour

Middle Rd.

PAGET

Somerset Br.

Harbour Rd.

WARWICK

Spring
Benny's
Bay

Middle Rd.

Little Sound

Middle Rd.

South Shore Rd.

West Whale
Bay

Warwick Long Bay

SOUTHAMPTON

Gibbs Hill
Lighthouse

Horseshoe
Bay

Church
Bay

0 —————————— 2 miles

0 —————————— 3 km

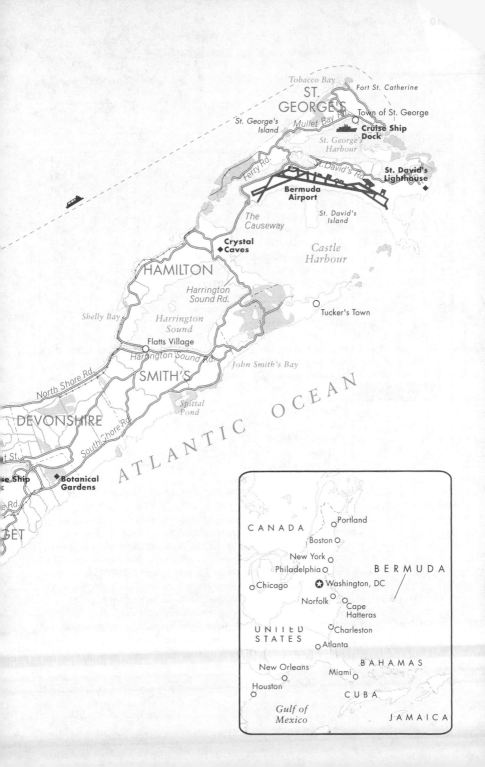

ST. GEORGE'S	
	Bermuda's original capital (from the early 17th century until 1815), St. George's was named as a UNESCO World Heritage Site in 2000 and is a must for history buffs. Settled in 1609, it was the second English settlement in the New World, after Jamestown, Virginia. Today its cobbled streets, narrow alleys, and walled lanes are packed with British-style pubs, seafood restaurants, boutiques, museums, forts, churches, and historic sights, including King's Square, where cedar replicas of the stocks, pillory, and ducking stool once used to punish criminals now serve as props. For visitors more occupied with the here and now, St. Georges's offers magnificent beaches, challenging golf courses, an affluent area of residential estates, fine-art galleries, and lively taverns. When cruise ships are in port, St. George's can be overflowing with visitors and its charm is somewhat obscured. Brave the crowds to take in its many attractions, and try to come back for an after-supper stroll.
SANDYS	
	Pronounced *Sands,* Sandys parish in the West End of Bermuda encompasses Somerset, Boaz, and Ireland islands, bucolic areas of nature reserves, wooded areas, and beautiful bays and harbors. When you cross Somerset Bridge—the smallest working drawbridge in the Western Hemisphere—you are, as Bermudians say, "up the country." It is a rural area of small farms and open space, craggy coastlines, gentle beaches, and parks and nature preserves—unspoiled, romantic Bermuda. The biggest attraction in Sandys is the Royal Naval Dockyard, a former bastion of the Royal British Navy and now a major tourist center with a maritime museum, shopping arcade, crafts market, and restaurants and pubs. On most days you can watch artisans at work on their cedar work, quilts, candles, banana-leaf dolls, miniature furniture, hand-painted fabrics, and more at the Bermuda Arts Center, or you can create your own island-inspired souvenirs at Bermuda Clayworks Pottery. Sandys is isolated, so if your Bermuda vacation plan is to shop or bop 'til you drop then base yourself in Hamilton and visit Sandys on a Tuesday evening for "Destination Dockyard," a weekly street festival.

SOUTHAMPTON	
	At certain points on this long, narrow strip of land, such as high on St. Anne's Road, you can see the ocean on both the northern and southern sides of the country. If you plan to spend plenty of time in that water or on the beach by day and then socializing by night, Southampton Parish with its beautiful pink sandy beaches, manicured golf courses, and elegant resorts that line them is the best place to stay. With clear water, a ⅓-mi crescent of pink sand, a vibrant social scene, and the uncluttered backdrop of South Shore Park, Horseshoe Bay Beach is Southampton's best beach and has everything you could ask of a Bermudian beach. Although the nightlife here is not as varied as Hamilton, resorts like the Fairmont Southampton Princess and the Wyndham Resort attract a lively mix of tourists and locals, especially on Sunday nights.
WARWICK	
	Warwick is somewhat isolated from restaurants and nightlife but there are enough long, sandy beaches and sporting activities to keep you entertained here for a few days. Warwick's claim to fame is Warwick Long Bay, Bermuda's longest beach, with a coral outcrop close to shore. This beach is rarely crowded, so it's a great place to chill out with a book and a picnic. If you're feeling a little more energetic, you can avail of some of the Warwick's various sports offerings, like hiking, horseback riding, diving, bird-watching, and golfing.
PAGET	
	Paget has some of Bermuda's best south-shore beaches, resort hotels, and dining choices. It's also a stone's throw from Hamilton, and central to ferry and bus connections, so it's a great place to stay. Paget has excellent seaside resorts and hotels, but you'll also find plenty of apartments, B&Bs, cottages, and inns for all budgets. Be sure to explore Paget's charming neighborhoods with distinctly Bermudian architecture and the coastline along South Road, and don't miss the Botanical Gardens and Paget Marsh.
PEMBROKE	
	Bermuda's most populous parish is home to the island's capital city of Hamilton, a small bustling city, referred to as "the town" by locals. Here you'll find the island's greatest concentration of restaurants, shops, art galleries, and historic and cul-

tural sights. You can easily make your way around on foot and there's a lot to see. Great photo op's include Fort Hamilton, Front Street, City Hall, and the Cathedral of the Most Holy Trinity. The Bermuda Underwater Exploration Institute is just a 15 minute walk from the town.

DEVONSHIRE

Devonshire Parish may be the geographical center of the island, but it is far off the beaten track when compared to the attractions and distractions of Hamilton and St. George's. With rolling green hills and elegant seaside estates, this sleepy parish has few of Bermuda's major attractions but it's a great place to get away from it all, to walk and wander, and to base yourself for exploring the East and West ends. Devonshire's draws include Ocean View Golf Course, the landmark Old Devonshire Church, Freer Cox Memorial and Firefly nature reserves, and the Montpelier Arboretum. The parish is also home to Bermuda's largest venue, the National Sports Centre, which hosts local sporting events as well as large-scale musical performances.

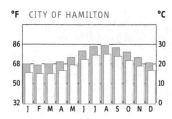

°F CITY OF HAMILTON °C

Bermuda's Department of Tourism promotes two seasons: "beach and sizzle" (summer) and "golf and spa" (winter). In summer, the island teems with activity; hotel barbecues and evening dances complement daytime sightseeing trips, and public beaches never close. The pace slows considerably in the off season (November through March). A few hotels and restaurants close; some of the sightseeing, dive, snorkeling, and water-skiing boats are dry-docked; and only taxis operate tours of the island. Most hotels remain open, however, and slash their rates by as much as 40%. The weather at this time of year is often perfect for golf and tennis, and you can still rent boats, tour the island, and take advantage of sunny days and uncrowded beaches, shops, restaurants, and walking tours.

Climate

Bermuda has a remarkably mild climate that seldom sees extremes of either heat or cold. In winter (December through March), temperatures range from around 55°F at night to 70°F in early afternoon. High, blustery winds can make the air feel cooler, however, as can Bermuda's high humidity. The hottest part of the year is between May and mid-October, when temperatures generally range from 75°F to 85°F. It's not uncommon for the temperature to reach 90°F in July and August. The summer months are somewhat drier, but rainfall is spread fairly evenly throughout the year. Bermuda depends solely on rain for its supply of fresh water, so residents usually greet a summer shower as "good tank water" in reference to the tanks where rain water is stored beneath many of the houses. In August and September, hurricanes moving north from the Caribbean sometimes batter the island and cause flight delays.

🗲 Forecasts **Weather Channel Connection** ☏ 900/932–8437 95¢ per minute ⊕ www.weather.com. The **Bermuda Weather Service** can be found at ⊕ www.weather.bm.

The chart above shows average daily high and low temperatures for Bermuda.

QUINTESSENTIAL BERMUDA

Pink Sandy Beaches

Bermuda's sand is white with a faint blush, because, as the locals say, it is so romantic here that even the sand is blushing. Although this may be true, it could also be said that the trademark fine pink sand is a result of the red-shell particles (from microscopic creatures called foraminifera that live on the island's reefs), calcium carbonate, and bits of crushed coral mixing together with sand. Although there is no official "pinkometer" to measure the various beaches, the pink does appear more noticeable along the South Shore. When locals say they are going to the beach, they are usually referring to Horseshoe Bay; the island's flagship beach curving gently along the South Shore with fine, pink sand and a vibrant social scene. Bermudians are friendly and happy to share their favorite beach with visitors, so get your towel.

A Knee Breeze

Bermuda shorts may well be the most recognizable symbol of the island, even more so than the Bermuda Triangle. Originally part of a military uniform, these flamboyantly dyed shorts worn with knee socks and a blazer are a source of constant amusement to visitors but a matter of pride to locals. New York's 2005 Fashion Week declared Bermuda shorts a summer necessity for men and women, teens and adults, but in Bermuda the shorts are worn by businessmen, and businessmen only. Join in this local tradition and flash a little leg, but play by the rules. You'll be frowned upon if seen in a pair of check-pattern American interpretations. Real Bermudas are characterized by their fabric and styling—linen or wool blends, hitting 3 inches above the knee. Bermudas start at about US$55 a pair and a good place to find a genuine pair is the English Sports Shop on Front Street.

Only 500 mi east of the United States, Bermuda is so close, and yet *so* far away. You don't have to set up shop on this little 21-square-mi island to fully experience its serene, even pace of life. Just sample a few local pleasures and you'll be kicking back like a true Bermudian in no time.

Cup Match

On the Thursday and Friday before the first Monday in August, Bermuda celebrates a two-day holiday to allow its residents to watch Cup Match, an annual cricket game pitting the West End against the East End. Cup Match fever begins in the weeks leading up to the event, when ribbons and flags begin to appear on the island's cars and houses in either the blue and light blue of St. George's or the red and navy of Somerset. Although cricket is taken very seriously, the event itself is an excuse to party. If you want a memorable, truly Bermudian experience, attend a game yourself. The carnival atmosphere and excited antics of spectators is as entertaining as the cricket. Feeling lucky? Check out one of the biggest attractions for Cup Match, the Crown & Anchor tent, and try your hand at the only legal betting event on Bermuda's calendar—a gambling game brought here by British sailors in the 19th century.

Johnny Barnes

"Good morning. I love you!" he calls, waving and smiling. Many reply "Good morning, Mr. Barnes. Love you too, darlin'." And they mean it. Standing on the Crow Lane roundabout at the entrance to the City of Hamilton every weekday morning from about 6 to 10, come rain or shine, an eccentric retired bus driver named Johnny Barnes greets drivers on their way into town. Johnny first started waving to morning commuters more than two decades ago and now Bermudians rely on Johnny for their early morning smile, knowing that a wave and a "God bless you" are sure to lighten even the worst Monday morning mood. Johnny is always willing to chat with tourists, but be careful, it can be hazardous crossing the busy thoroughfare in the mornings to reach him. You may have to be content with just a wave and an "I love you."

IF YOU LIKE

Golf

Bermuda is famous for its golf courses and close enough to the United States and Canada to be pitched as "putting distance" from the eastern seaboard. The rich and famous are known to frolic on many of Bermuda's private courses such as the Mid-Ocean Club or Tucker's Point, while some of the public courses like Port Royal are world-renowned and popular with locals. The hotel courses can be surprisingly affordable: the golf course at the Fairmont Southampton Princess hotel is one of our favorites for golfers of all skill levels, and it won't break your piggy bank to play there for an afternoon.

- **Mid-Ocean Golf Club, Tucker's Town.** If you can find a way in via an introduction by a member, you'll find yourself on one of the most spectacular and elite courses on the island and in the world.

Many tracks have holes on the ocean or atop the seaside cliffs; they're wonderfully scenic, but the wind and that big natural water hazard can play havoc with your game.

- **Port Royal Golf Course, Southampton Parish.** Accessible, inexpensive, and overlooking gorgeous Whale Bay, this classic Bermudian public course is a Jack Nicklaus favorite, is flatter than most Bermudian layouts, and has a faithful weekend following among locals.

- **Fairmont Southampton Princess Golf Course, Southampton Parish.** Good for golfers of all abilities, this course is a good warm up for Bermuda's full-length courses, and an affordable afternoon's play.

- **Riddell's Bay Golf & Country Club.** You don't need to be a power hitter to score well on these relatively flat palm-lined fairways.

Nightlife

Visitors come to Bermuda for the sun, sand, and sights, and not so much to rave and rock until dawn. That said, the island does not go to sleep with the sun so there's plenty to see and do after dark, especially in summer. There are no casinos in Bermuda and only a few nightclubs, so most of the action takes place in the island's hotel bars, pubs, and lounges. Bars generally stay open until 1, and clubs close at 3 AM. It's a good idea to include dinner in your night's agenda, since there are no fast-food restaurants here to feed an after-hours salsa-steps-and-rum-swizzles appetite. Base yourself in the city of Hamilton for efficient fun.

- **The Beach** is a fun and noisy spot where you'll find hip DJs, a diverse mix of well-watered socializers, and cheap drinks. There's no cover charge and it's one of the few nightspots in Bermuda that stays hopping until 3 AM.

- The popular **Pickled Onion** is a little more sober and sophisticated, but never boring. Mingle with expatriots here and enjoy the view of the harbor, the good selection of cocktails, wine by the glass, and the lively sing-alongs to the hot summer entertainment.

- Be sure to test the nightlife options outside of town for a little low-key local fun. **The White Horse Tavern** in St. George's is a great place to visit for drinks on Tuesday nights after the nearby street festival. **Henry VII Restaurant & Bar** on South Road in Southampton is popular on summer Sundays, as is **The Cellar,** a pub and nightclub inside the Fairmont Southampton Princess.

Walking

Restricted to pedestrians, horseback riders, and cyclists (including scooters), the secluded 18-mile recreational **Railway Trail** runs the length of the island along the route of the old railway, with fabulous views of the coast along the way. One of our favorite sections of the trail starts near the Southampton Princess and ends up on Church Road by the Southampton Post Office. Pick up a copy of the "Bermuda Railway Trail Guide" at the Department of Tourism for other suggested routes. If you're visiting in May, you can work up a charitable sweat with the annual End-to-End Charity Walk that follows the Railway Trail route.

- **Spittal Pond Nature Reserve** is a 60-acre park with 25 species of waterfowl and lush scenic (unpaved) stretches to walk with less company than the Railway Trail.

- The stretches of sand dunes between **Horseshoe Bay** and **Warwick Long Bay** forming South Shore Park are a great place to explore with several small beaches along the walk.

- Let your nose lead your toes around the impressive grounds of the **Botanical Gardens**, a 36-acre heavenly scented paradise with a palm garden, a garden for the blind, a miniature forest, an aviary, and the "White House", the official residence of Bermuda's Premier.

- Stroll along the shaded paths of **Hog Bay Park** past agricultural fields, woodlands, a hillside dotted with dead cedars, past an ancient lime kiln, abandoned cottages, and down to the bay with fabulous views of the ocean.

Water Sports

More than any other factor, climate is what makes Bermuda so ideal for sports—both in the water and out. Warm clear water, reefs, shipwrecks, underwater caves, and a variety of coral and marine life combine to make Bermuda an ideal place for underwater exploration. The water sport favored by many Bermudians is to drop anchor, crack open a case of beer, and float the day away—an activity that should not be knocked until it is tried. But if water-skiing, kayaking, parasailing, snorkeling, or scuba diving are more to your liking, the crystal-clear waters of Bermuda offer endless opportunities.

- **9 Beaches.** Aquatic adventures at this relaxed resort include sunfishing, sailboarding, snorkeling, kiteboarding, kayaking, banana boats, jet skis, floating trampolines, climbing walls, and paddleboats. Try snuba—a hybrid of snorkeling and scuba—just so you can say you "snuba'd!"

- **Blue Water Divers Ltd.** First-time divers are in good hands here with lesson-and-dive packages (including equipment) for $99. The more adventurous can ride a diver-propulsion vehicle (DPV), which is like an underwater scooter, from the Elbow Beach Hotel location past a wreck and through caves and canyons.

- Swim, touch, feed, and play with bottlenose dolphins at **Dolphin Quest's** outdoor oceanic pools. If you're feeling adventurous you can ride underwater scooters alongside swimming dolphins.

GREAT ITINERARY

BERMUDA SHORTS: SEA, SAND, AND SIGHTS

Day 1: Horseshoe Bay Beach

You came for the pink sand so don't waste any time finding it! You could spend day one just wandering from beach to beautiful beach (the no. 7 bus takes you to and from the City of Hamilton) along Bermuda's South Shore or you could just pick one and park yourself for the day. Our pick is Horseshoe Bay Beach, with clear water, a ⅓-mi crescent of pink sand, a vibrant social scene, and the uncluttered backdrop of South Shore Park. Horseshoe Bay is a favorite with locals and visitors alike so it can be crowded but for good reason—unlike most other beaches here Horseshoe Bay has a snack bar, changing rooms, beach gear-rental facilities, and lifeguards. There are also some nice trails through the nearby park that will take you to more secluded coves. Bring a hat, plenty of water, and a light sweater if you plan to stay until evening. Don't forget a strong sunscreen for your skin and pride's sake; a bad sunburn and road rash (from skimming the road on a scooter!) are the most common—and obvious—ailments for Bermuda's visitors.

Day 2: City of Hamilton

Bermuda's capital, and the center of Bermudian life, this bustling little city has the all the makings for a great day of shopping, eating, and sightseeing, and a fun night of drinking, dancing, and more eating. Start your day outside the city at the Bermuda Underwater Exploration Institute where you can spend a few hours with shipwrecks, shells, and the amazing science of the sea, all without getting wet.

If the pretty little fish make you hungry you can stop for lunch at the onsite restaurant, La Coquille, and then head into town. It's about a fifteen minute walk into the city of Hamilton where you can easily spend a few hours strolling in and out of shops and galleries. You'll have lots of company though if there are cruise ships in the harbor. Be sure to visit Front St. and its colorful little alleyways, where you can catch your breath and even more souvenirs. We like to end our day with the fifteen minute-walk to Fort Hamilton—a must see for history buffs and a great spot for vacation photos—and then take a bus or taxi home to drop off our goodies, and gear up to explore the lively City of Hamilton by night.

Day 3: Town of St. George

No trip to Bermuda is complete without a visit to this historic town and UNESCO World Heritage Site. The Town of St. George is an outstanding example of an early English settlement in the New World, with old walled lanes and quaint alleys that beg to be explored. You can easily spend a day strolling the cobblestone streets and visiting museums, churches, forts, shops, and old English pubs. There's good shopping in King's Square, and Fort St. Catherine, on of the island's most impressive forts, is certainly worth a visit. Be sure to stop for a little snorkeling or snoozing in the snug Tobacco cove near Fort St. Catherine. The easternmost stretch of the Railway Trail starts west of the Town of St. George if you haven't walked enough already today.

Day 4: Dockyard

Once a British military fortress, and now a tourism and recreation center, the Royal Naval Dockyard offers a day of adventure and history. There are stunning views, a maritime museum, an arts center, a shopping area, and you can swim with dolphins at Dolphin Quest. You can hang out here for the whole day and have a hearty meal at one of the Dockyard's pubs or take the slow rumbling ferry past secluded coves and inlets to Watford Bridge from where you can explore Somerset Village and Somerset Bridge.

Day 5: Drive by Bermuda

One of the best ways to get to know Bermuda is by taking a long bicycle or scooter ride, and stopping at various sights along the way. You can also hire a taxi for a driving tour. Must see-sights include Gibb's Hill Lighthouse, for the best view of the island and a perfectly delightful afternoon tea; Fort Hamilton in Somerset; Verdmont House in Smith's; the Botanical Gardens in Paget; Paget Marsh; and the sections of the Railway Trail that take in Southampton and Sandy's Parish. A tour of the island outside its major communities will show you that there is so much more to Bermuda than pink sandy beaches.

TIPS

❶ The Portuguese man-of-war jellyfish looks like a small blue plastic bag floating on top of the waves but their sting is extremely painful and poisonous, so steer clear. Check the notice board at Horseshoe Bay for current jellyfish info.

❷ The only beaches here with lifeguards on duty are at the Horseshoe Bay, John Smith's Bay, and Clearwater beaches.

❸ The northern end of Court Street in the City of Hamilton is a little off the typical tourist trail so you'll find a few great local eateries and a taste of day-to-day Bermuda life. Be warned, this area is not advisable after dark.

❹ Try to make any sporting reservations before you arrive in Bermuda; chartered boats and golf tee-times are especially high in demand.

❺ The Bermuda Aquarium, Museum & Zoo in Flatt's Village is not to be missed if you're traveling with little ones. The nearby Bermuda Railway Museum is usually a hit too. Stop for lunch at Rustico's.

ON THE CALENDAR

ONGOING	Heritage, music, theater, dance, and sports festivals are scheduled year-round in Bermuda, and you can find great room-and-festival hotel deals if you shop around.
Mar.–Oct.	The Ceremony is usually performed twice monthly by the Bermuda Regiment Band, the Bermuda Islands Pipe Band with Dancers, and members of the Bermuda Pipe Band. The historic ceremony is performed alternately on Front Street in Hamilton, King's Square in St. George's, and Dockyard in the West End. There are no performances in August.
WINTER	Every few weeks usually sees an art opening at City Hall or an amateur performance of some kind at the Bermuda Musical and Dramatic Society ☎ 441/272–0848. The Bermuda Calendar, found in the Lifestyles section of the island's daily newspaper, *The Royal Gazette* ☎ 441/295–5881 and the weekly *Preview* magazine, often available at the airport or in hotels, will detail what is happening on the island during your stay. Entertainment Web sites Blackand-Coke.com ⊕ www.blackandcoke.com and Bermynet ⊕ www.bermynet.com offer visitors a glimpse of Bermuda's night, sporting, and cultural life.
Dec.	In the Christmas Boat Parade, lighted yachts and boats of many sizes float along in Hamilton Harbour, followed by a fireworks extravaganza. It usually takes place on the second Saturday of the month, though there may be a rain date scheduled. The parade draws thousands of spectators along Front Street (arrive early if you want to view it from here), at the Hamilton Princess, along Harbour Road or in the Harbour itself. A commentator and music accompany the parade at Front Street, though all the boats usually have their own music playing. Floats can range from the beautiful to the ridiculous to the satirical. In 2004 organizers estimated that the event drew the equivalent of nearly one-third the country's population as spectators.
	Father Christmas visits Front Street in the Hamilton Jaycees Santa Claus Parade, usually held the first Sunday in December. Santa is accompanied by marching bands, majorettes, and floats. He forgoes his sled, and instead rides high in a red fire truck while others in the parade toss candy to children in the crowd.
	The Bermuda Aquarium, Natural History Museum & Zoo ☎ 441/293–2727 also has an annual yuletide "do," with children's games, a crafts workshop, and a visit with Santa in the Zoo Garden.

	The **Bermuda National Trust Annual Christmas Walkabout in St. George's** ☎ 441/236–6483, a festive early evening open-house event, features traditional Christmas decorations, musicals in the State House, monologues at the Globe Hotel, and historic readings at the Town Hall.
	Boxing Day (December 26) is a public holiday, when you'll find a variety of sports events, and various Gombey dancing troupes performing around the island.
	St. George's New Year's Eve Celebration ☎ 441/297–1532 in King's Square and on Ordnance Island has food stalls, rides for children, and continuous entertainment by local musicians. A midnight countdown and dropping of the "onion" are followed by fireworks.
Jan.	**Bermuda International Race Weekend** ☎ 441/236–6086 kicks off on the third weekend of the month. The event begins Friday night with the popular Front Street Mile. It also includes marathon and half-marathon races and a fitness-and-charity 10-km (6.2 mi) walk. Top international runners participate, but most races are open to all.
	Thousands of residents attend performances put on by the **Bermuda Festival** ☎ 441/235–1291. This two-month program attracts internationally known artists for concerts, dance, and theater.
	The **Annual Regional Bridge Tournament** ☎ 441/295–5161, sponsored by the Bermuda Unit of the American Contract Bridge League, is held at the Fairmont Southampton Princess the last week of January.
	At the **Annual Photographic Exhibition** ☎ 441/292–3824, held during the third week of the month in the Bermuda Society of the Arts gallery, you can see the work of local amateur and professional photographers, including many underwater shots.
Jan.–Mar.	The **Regimental Musical Display** ☎ 441/238–2470 is a captivating re-creermuda Regiment Band and the Bermuda Islands Pipe Band with Dancers.
Feb.	The **Bermuda International Open Chess Tournament** ☎ 441/238–2313 is open to both residents and visitors
	The **Annual Bermuda Rendezvous Bowling Tournament** ☎ 441/236–5290, sanctioned by the ABC and WIBC, is open to all bowlers. Cash prizes are awarded.

SPRING	
Mar.	The Bermuda All Breed Championship Dog Shows and Obedience Trials ☎ 441/291–1426 draw dog lovers from far and wide to the Botanical Gardens in Paget. The event is held again in November.

The Bermuda Super Senior Invitational Tennis Tournament ☎ 441/296–0834 is a USTA-sanctioned event held at the Coral Beach & Tennis Club in Paget. It is held during the second week in March.

See a range of equestrian events at the Bermuda Horse & Pony Association Spring Show ☎ 441/234–0485, including dressage, jumping, Western, and driving classes, at the National Equestrian Centre.

The Bermuda Men's Amateur Golf Championship ☎ 441/295–9972 is played at the Mid Ocean Club in Tucker's Town.

The Bermuda Cat Fanciers Association Championship Cat Show ☎ 441/238–0112 or 441/295–5723 features pedigree felines and household pets judged at various locations. Contact Morag Smith or Diana Plested. |
| Mar.–Apr. | The Palm Sunday Walk ☎ 441/236–6483 is an annual stroll of 6 to 8 mi. A different route is taken each year.

Good Friday is a public holiday and traditionally a kite-flying day. Bermudians usually make special Bermuda kites out of tissue paper, glue, and wooden sticks, and celebrate with fish cakes on hot cross buns.

Enjoy a spectacular display of locally made kites at the Bermuda Kite Festival ☎ 441/295–0729, held at Horseshoe Bay in Southampton. |
| Apr. | The Annual Exhibition ☎ 441/236–4201, similar to a county or state fair, brings entertainment, exhibits, and plays reflective of Bermuda's agricultural and cultural heritage to the Botanical Gardens in Paget. The three-day event is usually held the third weekend in April. Locals know it best as the "Ag Show," short for "Agricultural Exhibition," a name changed to reflect the show's broadened horizons.

The Peppercorn Ceremony ☎ 441/297–1532 Corporation of St. George's celebrates—amid great pomp and circumstance, including a spectacular march by the Bermuda Regiment—the payment of one peppercorn in rent to the government by the Masonic Lodge of St. George No. 200 of the Grand Lodge of Scotland for its headquarters in the Old State House in St. George's. |

	The **XL Capital Bermuda Open** ☎ 441/296–2554 is an ATP Tour, USTA-sanctioned event of the world's top professionals.
	The **Annual Fun Run/Walk Around Harrington Sound** ☎ 441/293–7074 invites walkers, joggers, runners, bikers, rollerbladers—whatever—to go the 7- to 8-mi distance around the Sound.
	The popular seven-day **Bermuda International Film Festival** ☎ 441/293–3456, ⊕ www.bermudafilmfest.bm screens independent films in three theaters, including the winners of many other festivals, world premieres, and the work of Bermudian cineasts. Filmmakers are on hand to answer questions, and a movie celebrity of some sort is flown in to participate in the judges' panel. The festival usually begins the second week of April.
Apr.–May	The **Garden Club of Bermuda** ☎ 441/295–9155 leads tours through private houses and gardens.
	International Race Week ☎ 441/295–2214 pits Bermudians against sailors from around the world in a series of races on the Great Sound. Contact the Sailing Secretary of the Royal Bermuda Yacht Club.
May	May is **Bermuda Heritage Month** ☎ 441/292–9447, when a host of commemorative, cultural, and sporting activities is scheduled. The climax is Bermuda Day (May 24), a public holiday that includes a parade to the National Stadium, a cycling race, a half-marathon (13 mi) for Bermuda residents only, and Bermuda dinghy races in St. George's Harbour. Traditionally, Bermuda Day is also the first day of the year that locals go swimming, swearing the water is too cold for swimming before that—though most visitors don't seem to mind that kind of "cold."
	The **Bermuda End-to-End Scenic Railway Trail Walk for Charities** is a terrific way to see the island and meet active residents. The 26-mi course traverses almost the length of the country, mostly via the old Railway Trail, showcasing a Bermuda that many do not get to see. It begins in King's Square, St. George's, and finishes with a range of festivities at the Royal Naval Dockyard. An alternative, 15-mi course (middle-to-end) begins at Albuoy's Point, Hamilton. You can sign up 30 minutes before either starting point.
	The **Bermuda Senior Amateur Championships for Men and Ladies** ☎ 441/295–9972 are played on a different course each year. Women must be at least 50 years old, men at least 55.

SUMMER	**ZooDoo Day** ☎ 441/293–7074 at the Bermuda Aquarium, Museum & Zoo has free admission, fun, games, and gift stalls.
June	For **Queen Elizabeth II's Birthday,** a public holiday in mid-June, military marching bands parade down Hamilton's Front Street. The **Bermuda Angler's Club International Light Tackle Tournament** ☎ 441/296–4767 days, 441/236–6565 evenings, held the first or second week of the month, draws a large crowd to its 5 PM weigh-ins. Free **Open Air Pops Concerts** ☎ 441/238–1108 are presented by the Bermuda Philharmonic Society at King's Square, St. George's, and the Clocktower Mall at Dockyard. The **Bermuda Amateur Stroke Play Championship for Men and Ladies** ☎ 441/295–9972 are simultaneous events played at the Port Royal Golf Course. Men and women play 72 and 54 holes, respectively. **Harbour Nights,** a street festival featuring Bermudian artists, crafts, Gombey dancers, face painting, and the like, takes place every Wednesday night in summer on Front Street in the City of Hamilton. The **Flatts Festival** (scheduled to take place in Flatts on Monday nights during the summer of 2006), **Destination Dockyard** (scheduled on Tuesday in the Royal Naval Dockyard) and **Heritage Nights** (scheduled on Tuesday in St. George's) are summer street festivals which emulate the highly successful Harbour Nights.
July	Played at the Mid-Ocean Golf Cluband Port Royal golf course, the **Atlantic International Junior Championship** ☎ 441/295–5111 is a 72-hole junior golf tournament.
July–Aug.	The **Cup Match Cricket Festival** ☎ 441/234–0327 or 441/297–0374 is a two-day festival centered on the match between arch rivals Somerset and St. George's cricket clubs. Locals sport red and blue if they are Somerset fans, and blue and a lighter blue if they are St. George's fans. The festival is held on the weekend of Emancipation Day, a public holiday, either the last Thursday and Friday in July or the first Thursday and Friday in August. It's considered a highlight of the Bermuda calendar; thousands either watch the game or go camping for the long weekend. The **Sea Horse Anglers' Club Annual Bermuda Billfish Tournament** ☎ 441/292–7272 is a favorite among fishermen.

	Aug.	Landlubbers in homemade contraptions compete in the hilarious **Non-Mariners Race** ☎ 441/236–3683 in Mangrove Bay. If your contraption floats, you are disqualified.
		The **Byron Lee Soca Show** also usually takes place in August. Featuring soca legend Byron Lee and his band the Dragonaires, the show, held at Tiger Bay in St. George's, can draw crowds of up to 2,000 and the diversity of the crowd can be startling—families with small children mix happily among partying teenagers and older Bermudians, who sometimes bring their own deck chairs to relax among the dancing crowd. Tickets can usually be bought at the music store Music Box ☎ 441/295–4839, and food and drinks can be purchased at the show.
FALL	Sept.	**Labour Day** brings a number of activities, including a march from Union Square in Hamilton to Bernard Park. Local entertainers and food stalls selling local fare are part of the festivities.
		The **Bermuda Mixed Foursomes Amateur Golf Championship** ☎ 441/295–9972 is a 36-stroke play competition for couples at Port Royal Golf Course. Handicap limit: men 24, ladies 36.
		The **Annual Bermuda Triathlon** ☎ 441/293–2765 is open to visiting and local teams who compete in a 1-mi swim, 15-mi cycle, and 6-mi run.
		The **Bermuda Masters International Golf Classic** ☎ 800/648–1136 is played at Port Royal and Castle Harbour.
	Oct.	The **Bermuda Music Festival** brings the best of Bermudian and International entertainers together for a weekend of jazz, folk, pop, and gospel. Tickets can be purchased online at ⊕ www.bermudamusicfestival.com
		The **Bermuda Culinary Arts Festival** ⊕ www.bermudatourism.com/culinaryfest is a long weekend celebration that includes demonstrations, wine tastings, and lots of food.

Nov.	**Remembrance Day** is a public holiday in memory of Bermuda's and its allies' fallen soldiers. A parade with Bermudian, British, and U.S. military units, the Bermuda Police, and war-veterans' organizations takes place on Front Street in Hamilton. The **Reconvening of Parliament** ☎ 441/292–7408, on the first Friday in November, is preceded by the arrival of His Excellency the Governor, in plumed hat and full regalia, at the Cabinet Building in Hamilton. The governor then reads the Speech from the Throne, a speech detailing new policies and initiatives or the direction that the government wants to take in the coming year. Elected officials from both the Senate and the House of Assembly accompany the governor, often in splendid hats themselves. Arrive by 10:30 to secure a place to stand. The **Bermuda Four Ball Stroke Play Amateur Championships for Men and Ladies** ☎ 441/295–9972 are simultaneous events at the Port Royal Golf Course. The **World Rugby Classic** ☎ 441/295–6574 ⊕ www.worldrugby.bm pits international rugby players against the best players from Bermuda in a series of matches at the **National Sports Center** ✉ Frog La., Devonshire, while the audience celebrates in the stands.

SMART TRAVEL TIPS

ADDRESSES

The 180 islands that compose Bermuda
are divided into 9 parishes: Sandys (pro-
nounced Sands), Southampton, Warwick,
Paget, Pembroke, Devonshire, Smith's,
Hamilton, and St. George's. Their import
is pretty much historical these days,
although they often appear on addresses
following or in lieu of the street. It can
get confusing, however, since Hamilton
is both a city and a parish. The City of
Hamilton is actually in Pembroke Parish.
St. George's is a city within the parish of
the same name. We indicate Hamilton
Parish and St. George's Parish when we
refer to a property that falls outside the
respective city proper.

Although the numbering of houses is becoming more common, many houses still
are known only by their picturesque
names, and buildings in Hamilton are
numbered rather whimsically. In fact,
some Front Street buildings have two
numbers, one of them a historic address
that might not relate to the building's
present location. Ask a local for direc-
tions but be sure to say "Hello, how are
you?" first.

AIR TRAVEL

Nonstop service to Bermuda is available
year-round on major airlines from Atlanta,
Boston, Newark (NJ), New York City,
Washington, D.C., Baltimore, Philadelphia, Toronto, and London, and season-
ally from Miami, Charlotte, Orlando,
Detroit, and Halifax. Travelers from Australia and New Zealand must fly to
Bermuda via London, New York, or
Toronto. Most flights arrive around noon,
making for particularly long waits to get
through immigration; however, British Airways flights, and one American Airlines
flight from New York, arrive in the
evening. Fares from New York City may
be found for under $300 on some of the
budget airlines but the average price is
closer to $500 and can be as high as $800
in peak season, whereas fares from
Toronto are typically about $600, and
those from Gatwick start at $700.

BOOKING

When you book, **look for nonstop flights** and **remember that "direct" flights stop at least once.** Try to avoid connecting flights, which require a change of plane. Two airlines may operate a connecting flight jointly, so ask whether your airline operates every segment of the trip; you may find that the carrier you prefer flies you only part of the way. To find more booking tips and to check prices and make online flight reservations, log on to www.fodors.com.

CARRIERS

American flies nonstop to Bermuda twice daily from New York and twice a week from Miami during high season, April through October. Frequency drops from November to March. Continental flies twice daily from Newark, New Jersey. Delta has one daily flight from Atlanta and one from Boston. US Airways flies daily from New York, nonstop in high season, connecting in Philadelphia during low season. It also offers year-round service from Philadelphia and seasonal nonstop flights from Boston, Washington, D.C., and Charlotte. Air Canada has one daily flight from Toronto, plus a weekly seasonal flight from Halifax. British Airways flies in from London's Gatwick Airport four times per week in high season and three times per week in low season. USA 3000 is the best bet for budget travel and flies twice weekly from Newark and from Baltimore year-round. Flight regularity is subject to rapid change and airlines recommend that travelers check their Web sites for up-to-the-minute information.

🛪 Major Airlines **Air Canada** ☎ 888/247-2262 ⊕ www.aircanada.com. **American** ☎ 800/433-7300 ⊕ www.aa.com. **Continental** ☎ 800/231-0856 ⊕ www.continental.com. **Delta Airlines** ☎ 800/241-4141 ⊕ www.delta.com. **US Airways** ☎ 800/428-4322 ⊕ www.usairways.com. **USA 3000** ☎ 877/872-3000 ⊕ www.usa3000.com.
🛪 From the U.K. **British Airways** ☎ 0181/897-4000 ⊕ www.ba.com.

CHECK-IN & BOARDING

Flights to Bermuda are occasionally delayed or canceled due to high winds or crosswinds, particularly in the late summer and fall. Before you leave home for the airport, you should always **call to confirm whether or not there are Bermuda-bound delays.**

You should also **find out your carrier's check-in policy.** Plan to arrive at the airport about two hours before your scheduled departure time for flights from the United States or Canada and 2½ to 3 hours ahead for flights from other countries. You may need to arrive earlier if you're flying from one of the busier airports or during peak air-traffic times. To avoid delays at airport-security checkpoints, try not to wear any metal. Jewelry, belt and other buckles, steel-toe shoes, barrettes, and underwire bras are among the items that can set off detectors.

Assuming that not everyone with a ticket will show up, airlines routinely overbook planes. When everyone does, airlines ask for volunteers to give up their seats. In return, these volunteers usually get a several-hundred-dollar flight voucher, which can be used toward the purchase of another ticket, and are rebooked on the next flight out. If there are not enough volunteers, the airline must choose who will be denied boarding. Bermuda-bound travelers are rarely bumped, even during the island's busiest summer season. Instead, when overbooking occurs, some airlines switch to a larger aircraft. In the event that passengers are bumped, however, the first to go are typically those who checked in late and those flying on discounted tickets, so **check in and get to the gate as early as possible.**

Have your passport or government-issued photo ID handy. Bermuda is rather scrupulous about ID, and you'll be asked to show your passport when checking in and again when boarding.

At many airports outside Bermuda, travelers with only carry-on luggage can bypass the airline's front desk and check in at the gate. But in Bermuda, everyone checks in at the airline's front desk. U.S. customs has a desk here, too, so you won't have to clear customs at home when you land. Passengers returning to Britain or Canada will need to clear customs and immigration on arrival.

CUTTING COSTS

The least-expensive airfares to Bermuda are priced for round-trip travel and must usually be purchased in advance. Airlines generally allow you to change your return date for a fee; most low-fare tickets, however, are nonrefundable. It's smart to **call a number of airlines and check the Internet;** when you are quoted a good price, **book it on the spot**—the same fare may not be available the next day, or even the next hour. Always **check different routings** and look into using alternative airports. Also, price off-peak flights, which may be significantly less expensive than others. Travel agents, especially low-fare specialists (⇨ Discounts & Deals), are helpful.

Consolidators are another good source. They buy tickets for scheduled flights at reduced rates from the airlines, then sell them at prices that beat the best fare available directly from the airlines. Sometimes you can even get your money back if you need to return the ticket. Carefully read the fine print detailing penalties for changes and cancellations, purchase the ticket with a credit card, and **confirm your consolidator reservation with the airline.**

🛈 Consolidators AirlineConsolidator.com ☎ 888/468-5385 ⊕ www.airlineconsolidator.com; for international tickets. **Best Fares** ☎ 800/576-8255 or 800/576-1600 ⊕ www.bestfares.com; $59.90 annual membership. **Cheap Tickets** ☎ 800/377-1000 or 888/922-8849 ⊕ www.cheaptickets.com. **Expedia** ☎ 800/397-3342 or 404/728-8787 ⊕ www.expedia.com. **Hotwire** ☎ 866/468-9473 or 920/330-9418 ⊕ www.hotwire.com. **Now Voyager Travel** ✉ 45 W. 21st St., 5th floor, New York, NY 10010 ☎ 212/459-1616 🖷 212/243-2711 ⊕ www.nowvoyagertravel.com. **Onetravel.com** ⊕ www.onetravel.com. **Orbitz** ☎ 888/656-4546 ⊕ www.orbitz.com. **Priceline.com** ⊕ www.priceline.com. **Travelocity** ☎ 888/709-5983, 877/282-2925 in Canada, 0870/111-7060 in the U.K. ⊕ www.travelocity.com.

ENJOYING THE FLIGHT

State your seat preference when purchasing your ticket, and then repeat it when you confirm and when you check in. For more legroom, you can request one of the few emergency-aisle seats at check-in, if you are capable of lifting at least 50 pounds—a Federal Aviation Administration requirement of passengers in these seats. Seats behind a bulkhead also offer more legroom, but they don't have underseat storage. Don't sit in the row in front of the emergency aisle or in front of a bulkhead, where seats may not recline.

Ask the airline whether a snack or meal is served on the flight. If you have dietary concerns, **request special meals when booking.** These can be vegetarian, low-cholesterol, or kosher, for example. It's a good idea to pack some healthful snacks and a small (plastic) bottle of water in your carry-on bag. On long flights, try to maintain a normal routine, to help fight jet lag. At night, **get some sleep.** By day, **eat light meals, drink water** (not alcohol), and **move around the cabin** to stretch your legs. For additional jet-lag tips consult *Fodor's FYI: Travel Fit & Healthy* (available at bookstores everywhere).

Smoking policies vary from carrier to carrier. Many airlines prohibit smoking on all of their flights; others allow smoking only on certain routes or certain departures. Ask your carrier about its policy.

FLYING TIMES

Flying time to Bermuda from New York, Newark, Boston, Philadelphia, and Baltimore is about 2 hours; from Atlanta, 2¼ hours; from Toronto, 3 hours; and 7 hours from London Gatwick.

HOW TO COMPLAIN

If your baggage goes astray or your flight goes awry, complain right away. Most carriers require that you **file a claim immediately.** The Aviation Consumer Protection Division of the Department of Transportation publishes *Fly-Rights,* which discusses airlines and consumer issues and is available online. You can also find articles and information on mytravelrights.com, the Web site of the nonprofit Consumer Travel Rights Center.

🛈 Airline Complaints Aviation Consumer Protection Division ✉ U.S. Department of Transportation C 75, Room 4107, 400 7th St. SW, Washington, DC 20590 ☎ 202/366-2220 ⊕ airconsumer.ost.dot.gov. **Federal Aviation Administration Consumer Hotline** ✉ for inquiries: FAA, 800 Independence Ave. SW, Washington, DC 20591 ☎ 800/322-7873 ⊕ www.faa.gov.

ORTS & TRANSFERS

Bermuda's gateway is Bermuda International Airport (BDA), on the East End of the island, approximately 9 mi from Hamilton and 17 mi from Somerset.

🛪 **Bermuda International Airport (BDA)** ✉ 2 Kindley Field Rd., St. George's ☎ 441/293-1640 ⊕ www.bermudaairport.com.

TRANSFERS

Taxis, readily available outside the arrivals gate, are the usual and most convenient way to leave the airport. The approximate fare (not including tip) to Hamilton is $28; to St. George's, $15; to south-shore hotels, $35; and to Sandys (Somerset), $40. A surcharge of 25¢ is added for each piece of luggage stored in the trunk or on the roof. Fares are 25% higher between midnight and 6 AM and all day on Sunday and public holidays. Depending on traffic, the driving time to Hamilton is about 30 minutes; to Sandys, about one hour.

Bermuda Hosts Ltd. provides transportation to hotels and guest houses aboard air-conditioned 6- to 25-seat vans and buses. Reservations are recommended.

🛪 **Bermuda Hosts Ltd.** ☎ 441/293-1334 🖷 441/ 293-1335. **The Bermuda Industrial Union Taxi Co-op** ☎ 441/292-4476. **Bermuda Taxi Radio Cabs** ☎ 441/295-4141. **Island Wide Taxi Services** ☎ 441/ 292-5600. **Sandys Taxi Service** ☎ 441/234-2344.

DUTY-FREE SHOPPING

Although you can certainly find discounts on china, crystal, woolens, and other European imports, duty-free shopping in Bermuda is limited. To qualify for duty-free (or in-bond) liquor prices, you'll have to buy at least two 1-liter or five 75-centiliter bottles. However, each U.S. citizen (21 and older) may only bring back 1 liter of alcohol duty-free. You can arrange for duty-free liquor you buy at stores to be delivered to the airport, or you can purchase it at the airport itself.

BIKE TRAVEL

You'll be in the minority if you choose to pedal around Bermuda, since most two-wheelers on the island are mopeds. Traffic and high winds can make biking on island roads dangerous in winter. In addition, steep hills and winding roads (particularly those going north–south) mean that bikers need a lot of pedal power. However cycling is a popular pastime in Bermuda, and events like the Conyers Dill & Pearman Grand Prix in September are becoming increasingly popular with amateur cyclists who like to combine a holiday with some high-class racing. Bicycling on the Railway Trail, which is closed to vehicular traffic, is also particularly rewarding. The Bermuda Railway Trail Guide is free at all Visitors Service Bureaus. Day rates for rentals range from $15 to $25. Try to reserve bikes a few days in advance.

BIKES IN FLIGHT

Most airlines accommodate bikes as luggage, provided they are dismantled and boxed; check with individual airlines about packing requirements. Some airlines sell bike boxes, which are often free at bike shops, for about $15 (bike bags can be considerably more expensive). International travelers often can substitute a bike for a piece of checked luggage at no charge; otherwise, the cost is about $100. U.S. and Canadian airlines charge $40–$80 each way.

BOAT & FERRY TRAVEL

The Bermuda Ministry of Transport maintains excellent, frequent, and on-time ferry service from Hamilton to Paget and Warwick (the pink line), Somerset and the Dockyard in the West End (the blue line), Rockaway in Southampton (the green line), and, weekdays in summer only, the Dockyard and St. George's (the orange line).

FARES & SCHEDULES

A one-way adult fare to Paget or Warwick is $2.50; to Somerset, the Dockyard, or St. George's, $4. The last departures are at 9:45 PM from mid-April through mid-November, 9 PM from mid-November through mid-April. Sunday ferry service is limited and ends around 7 PM. You can bring a bicycle onboard free of charge, but you'll pay $4 extra to take a motor scooter to Somerset or the Dockyard, and scooters are not allowed on the smaller Paget and Warwick ferries. Neither bikes nor scooters are allowed on ferries to St. George's.

Discounted one-, three-, four-, and seven-day passes are available for use on both ferries and buses. They cost $12, $28, $35, and $45 respectively. Monthly passes are also offered at $55. The helpful ferry operators can answer questions about routes and schedules and can even help get your bike on board. Schedules are published in the phone book, posted at each landing, and are also available at the Ferry Terminal, Central Bus Terminal, Visitor Services Bureaus, and most hotels.

Ministry of Transport, Department of Marine and Ports Services Hamilton Ferry Terminal: ✉ 8 Front St., near Queen St. ☎ 441/295-4506 ⊕ www.seaexpress.bm.

BUSINESS HOURS

BANKS & OFFICES
Most branches of the Bank of Bermuda are open weekdays from 9 to 4:30 and Saturday from 11 to 1. All branches of the Bank of Butterfield are open Monday through Thursday from 9 to 3:30 and Friday from 9 to 4:30. Bermuda Commercial Bank (at 43 Victoria Street in Hamilton) operates Monday through Thursday from 9:30 to 3 and Friday from 9:30 to 4:30. Capital G Bank (at 25 Reid Street in Hamilton) is open weekdays from 8:30 to 4:30 and Saturday from 8:30 to 3:30.

GAS STATIONS
Many gas stations are open daily from 7 AM to 9 PM, and a few stay open until midnight. The island's only 24-hour gas station is Esso City Auto Market in Hamilton, near the Bank of Butterfield, off Par-La-Ville Road.

MUSEUMS & SIGHTS
Hours vary greatly, but museums are generally open Monday through Saturday from 9 or 9:30 to 4:30 or 5. Some close on Saturday. Check with individual museums for exact hours.

PHARMACIES
Pharmacies are open Monday through Saturday from 8 AM to 6 or 8 PM, and sometimes Sunday from around 11 to 6 PM.

SHOPS
Most stores are open Monday through Saturday from around 9 until 5 or 6. Some

Hamilton stores keep evening cruise ships are in port. Dockyard are generally open Monday through day from 10 to 5, Sunday from 11 to 5. The Bermuda government recently made it legal for all stores to open on Sunday, although most shops have yet to take advantage of the change. Those that are open—mainly grocery stores and pharmacies—have abbreviated hours.

BUS TRAVEL
Bermuda's pink-and-blue buses travel the island from east to west. To find a bus stop outside Hamilton, look for either a stone shelter or a pink-and-blue-striped pole. For buses heading to Hamilton, the top of the pole is pink; for those traveling away from Hamilton, the top is blue. Remember to **wait on the proper side of the road.** Driving in Bermuda is on the left. Bus drivers will not make change, so **purchase tickets or discounted tokens** or carry plenty of coins.

In addition to public buses, private minibuses serve St. George's. The minibus fare depends upon the destination, but you won't pay more than $5. Minibuses, which you can flag down, drop you wherever you want to go in this parish. They operate daily from about 7:30 AM to 9 PM. Smoking is not permitted on buses.

FARES & SCHEDULES
Bermuda is divided into 14 bus zones, each about 2 mi long. Within the first three zones, the rate is $3 (coins only). For longer distances, the fare is $4.50. If you plan to travel by public transportation often, buy a booklet of tickets (15 14-zone tickets for $30, or 15 3-zone tickets for $20). You can also buy a few tokens, which, unlike tickets, are sold individually. Tickets, tokens, and one-, three-, four-, and seven-day adult passes ($12, $28, $35, and $45 respectively). Monthly passes are also on offer at $55 each. All bus passes are also good for ferry service and are available at the central bus terminal. Tickets and passes are also sold at the Visitors Service Bureau in Hamilton, post offices, and at many hotels and guest houses. Passes are accepted on both buses and ferries.

Hamilton buses arrive and depart from the Central Bus Terminal. A small kiosk here is open weekdays from 7:15 to 5:30, Saturday from 8:15 to 5:30, and Sunday and holidays from 9:15 to 4:45; it's the only place to buy money-saving tokens.

Buses run about every 15 minutes, except on Sunday, when they usually come every half hour or hour, depending on the route. Bus schedules, which also contain ferry timetables, are available at the bus terminal in Hamilton and at many hotels. The timetable also offers an itinerary for a do-it-yourself, one-day sightseeing tour by bus and ferry. Upon request, the driver will be happy to tell you when you've reached your stop. **Be sure to greet the bus driver when boarding**—it's considered rude in Bermuda to ask a bus driver a question, such as the fare or details on your destination, without first greeting him or her. Exact change for the buses is essential.

☎ Public Transport Bermuda Central Bus Terminal: ⌧ Washington and Church Sts., Hamilton ☎ 441/292-3851 ⊕ www.bermudabuses.com. **St. George's Minibus Service** ☎ 441/297-8199.

CAMERAS & PHOTOGRAPHY

Photo processing is very expensive in Bermuda, so **develop your film when you get home.** Photography is forbidden in the Senate Chamber, Sessions House, and in the courts, but the rest of Bermuda offers plenty of wonderful photo opportunities. Horseshoe Bay, the view from Gibb's Hill Lighthouse, and the small coves near Warwick Long Bay make lovely subjects. If you are driving a motor scooter along South Shore Road, you might be tempted to snap a picture of the southern beaches. Locals are usually very friendly and will not hesitate to take your photo if you ask. The *Kodak Guide to Shooting Great Travel Pictures* (available at bookstores everywhere) is loaded with tips.

☎ Photo Help Kodak Information Center ☎ 800/242-2424 ⊕ www.kodak.com.

EQUIPMENT PRECAUTIONS

Don't pack film and equipment in checked luggage, where it is much more susceptible to damage. X-ray machines used to view checked luggage are extremely pow-

erful and therefore are likely to ruin your film. Try to ask for hand inspection of film, which becomes clouded after repeated exposure to airport X-ray machines, and **keep videotapes and computer disks away from metal detectors.** Always **keep film, tape, and computer disks out of the sun.** Carry an extra supply of batteries, and be prepared to turn on your camera, camcorder, or laptop to prove to airport security personnel that the device is real.

FILM & DEVELOPING

Although a roll of color-print film costs about the same as in the United States ($7–$8 for a 36-exposure roll), developing that film is another story. If you're in a hurry to see what you shot, plan to dish out a whopping $28 per roll for 36 exposures, whether or not you choose speedy three-hour processing.

VIDEOS

Blank NTSC videotapes run about $3 each for six hours of tape and $4 for eight hours.

CAR TRAVEL

You cannot rent a car in Bermuda. Bermuda has strict laws governing against overcrowded roads, so even Bermudians are only allowed one car per household. A popular albeit somewhat dangerous alternative is to rent mopeds or scooters (⇨ Moped & Scooter Travel), which are better for negotiating the island's narrow roads.

CHILDREN IN BERMUDA

When children need a break from the beach or pool, there is plenty to see and do in Bermuda, from the carriage and maritime museums to the aquarium and botanical gardens. Places that are especially appealing to children are indicated by a rubber-duckie icon (🐤) in the margin.

BABYSITTING

For babysitters, check with your hotel desk. The charge averages around $15 per hour per child. These rates may go up after midnight and they may vary depending on the number of children. Sitters may expect paid transportation.

FLYING

If your children are two or older, **ask about children's airfares.** As a general rule, infants under two not occupying a seat fly at greatly reduced fares or even for free. But if you want to guarantee a seat for an infant, you have to pay full fare. Consider flying during off-peak days and times; most airlines will grant an infant a seat without a ticket if there are available seats. When booking, **confirm carry-on allowances** if you're traveling with infants. In general, for babies charged 10% to 50% of the adult fare you are allowed one carry-on bag and a collapsible stroller; if the flight is full, the stroller may have to be checked or you may be limited to less.

Experts agree that it's a good idea to use safety seats aloft for children weighing less than 40 pounds. Airlines set their own policies: if you use a safety seat, U.S. carriers usually require that the child be ticketed, even if he or she is young enough to ride free, because the seats must be strapped into regular seats. And even if you pay the full adult fare for the seat, it may be worth it, especially on longer trips. Do **check your airline's policy about using safety seats during takeoff and landing.** Safety seats are not allowed everywhere in the plane, so get your seat assignments as early as possible.

When reserving, **request children's meals or a freestanding bassinet** (not available at all airlines) if you need them. But note that bulkhead seats, where you must sit to use the bassinet, may lack an overhead bin or storage space on the floor.

FOOD

Kentucky Fried Chicken and Chester's Fried Chicken, within the Hamilton Ice Queen, a Bermudian burger joint, provide the island's only fast-food options, but children will have no trouble finding familiar menu items in welcoming settings, especially at casual restaurants like the Pickled Onion and the Hog Penny.

SUPPLIES & EQUIPMENT

Major American brands of baby formula, disposable diapers, and over-the-counter children's medications are widely available. However, prices are steep.

COMPUTERS ON THE ROAD

You should have no trouble bringing a laptop through customs into Bermuda, though you may have to open and turn it on for inspection by security officers. It would be a good idea to bring proof of purchase with you so you will not run into any difficulty bringing the computer back to the States, especially if it is a new machine.

Most hotels charge connection fees each time a laptop is hooked up to the Internet ($3 to $10), with additional charges (10¢ to 30¢ per minute) during the connection. The Fairmont Southampton and the Newstead Hotel both have fully equipped business centers where guests can use hotel computers for Internet access (connection charges still apply).

CONSUMER PROTECTION

Whether you're shopping for gifts or purchasing travel services, **pay with a major credit card** whenever possible, so you can cancel payment or get reimbursed if there's a problem (and you can provide documentation). If you're doing business with a particular company for the first time, **contact your local Better Business Bureau and the attorney general's offices** in your state and (for U.S. businesses) the company's home state as well. Have any complaints been filed? Finally, if you're buying a package or tour, always **consider travel insurance** that includes default coverage (⇨ Insurance).

♬ BBBs Council of Better Business Bureaus ✉ 4200 Wilson Blvd., Suite 800, Arlington, VA 22203 ☎ 703/276-0100 🖷 703/525-8277 ⊕ www.bbb.org.

CUSTOMS & DUTIES

When shopping, **keep receipts** for all purchases. Upon reentering your home country, **be ready to show customs officials what you've bought.** Pack purchases together in an easily accessible place. If you think a duty is incorrect, appeal the assessment. If you object to the way your clearance was handled, note the inspector's badge number. In either case, first ask to see a supervisor. If the problem isn't resolved, write to the appropriate authorities, beginning with the port director at your point of entry.

IN AUSTRALIA

Australian residents who are 18 or older may bring home A$400 worth of souvenirs and gifts (including jewelry), 250 cigarettes or 250 grams of cigars or other tobacco products, and 1,125 milliliters of alcohol (including wine, beer, and spirits). Residents under 18 may bring back A$200 worth of goods. Members of the same family traveling together may pool their allowances. Prohibited items include meat products. Seeds, plants, and fruits need to be declared upon arrival.

🛃 **Australian Customs Service** ⌖ Regional Director, Box 8, Sydney, NSW 2001 ☎ 02/9213-2000 or 1300/363263, 02/9364-7222 or 1800/803-006 quarantine-inquiry line 🖷 02/9213-4043 ⊕ www.customs.gov.au.

IN BERMUDA

On entering Bermuda, you can bring in duty-free up to 50 cigars, 200 cigarettes, and 1 pound of tobacco; 1 liter of wine and 1 liter of spirits; and other goods with a total maximum value of $30. To import plants, fruits, vegetables, or pets, you must get an import permit in advance from the Department of Environmental Protection. Merchandise and sales materials for use at conventions must be cleared with the hotel concerned before you arrive.

🛃 **Department of Environmental Protection** ⌖ HM 834, Hamilton HM CX ☎ 441/236-4201 🖷 441/232-0046 ⊕ www.animals.gov.bm.

IN CANADA

Canadian residents who have been out of Canada for at least seven days may bring in C$750 worth of goods duty-free. If you've been away fewer than seven days but more than 48 hours, the duty-free allowance drops to C$200. If your trip lasts 24 to 48 hours, the allowance is C$50. You may not pool allowances with family members. Goods claimed under the C$750 exemption may follow you by mail; those claimed under the lesser exemptions must accompany you. Alcohol and tobacco products may be included in the seven-day and 48-hour exemptions but not in the 24-hour exemption. If you meet the age requirements of the province or territory through which you reenter Canada, you may bring in, duty-free, 1.5 liters of wine

or 1.14 liters (40 imperial ounces) of liquor or 24 12-ounce cans or bottles of beer or ale. Also, if you meet the local age requirement for tobacco products, you may bring in, duty-free, 200 cigarettes and 50 cigars. Check ahead of time with the Canada Customs and Revenue Agency or the Department of Agriculture for policies regarding meat products, seeds, plants, and fruits.

You may send an unlimited number of gifts (only one gift per recipient, however) worth up to C$60 each duty-free to Canada. Label the package UNSOLICITED GIFT—VALUE UNDER $60. Alcohol and tobacco are excluded.

🛃 **Canada Customs and Revenue Agency** ✉ 2265 St. Laurent Blvd., Ottawa, Ontario K1G 4K3 ☎ 800/461-9999, 204/983-3500, or 506/636-5064 ⊕ www.ccra.gc.ca.

IN NEW ZEALAND

All homeward-bound residents may bring back NZ$700 worth of souvenirs and gifts; passengers may not pool their allowances, and children can claim only the concession on goods intended for their own use. For those 17 or older, the duty-free allowance also includes 4.5 liters of wine or beer; one 1,125-milliliter bottle of spirits; and either 200 cigarettes, 250 grams of tobacco, 50 cigars, or a combination of the three up to 250 grams. Meat products, seeds, plants, and fruits must be declared upon arrival to the Agricultural Services Department.

🛃 **New Zealand Customs** ✉ Head office: The Customhouse, 17–21 Whitmore St., Box 2218, Wellington ☎ 09/300-5399 or 0800/428-786 ⊕ www.customs.govt.nz.

IN THE U.K.

From countries outside the European Union, including Bermuda, you may bring home, duty-free, 200 cigarettes or 50 cigars; 1 liter of spirits or 2 liters of fortified or sparkling wine or liqueurs; 2 liters of still table wine; 60 milliliters of perfume; 250 milliliters of toilet water; plus £145 worth of other goods, including gifts and souvenirs. Prohibited items include meat products, seeds, plants, and fruits.

🛃 **HM Customs and Excise** ✉ Portcullis House, 21 Cowbridge Rd. E, Cardiff CF11 9SS ☎ 0845/010-

9000 or 0208/929-0152, 0208/929-6731 or 0208/910-3602 complaints ⊕ www.hmce.gov.uk.

IN THE U.S.

U.S. residents who have been out of the country for at least 48 hours may bring home, for personal use, $800 worth of foreign goods duty-free, as long as they haven't used the $800 allowance or any part of it in the past 30 days. This exemption may include 1 liter of alcohol (for travelers 21 and older), 200 cigarettes, and 100 non-Cuban cigars. Family members from the same household who are traveling together may pool their $800 personal exemptions. For fewer than 48 hours, the duty-free allowance drops to $200, which may include 50 cigarettes, 10 non-Cuban cigars, and 150 milliliters of alcohol (or 150 milliliters of perfume containing alcohol). The $200 allowance cannot be combined with other individuals' exemptions, and if you exceed it, the full value of all the goods will be taxed. Antiques, which the U.S. Bureau of Customs and Border Protection defines as objects more than 100 years old, enter duty-free, as do original works of art done entirely by hand, including paintings, drawings, and sculptures. This doesn't apply to folk art or handicrafts, which are in general dutiable.

You may also send packages home duty-free, with a limit of one parcel per addressee per day (except alcohol or tobacco products or perfume worth more than $5). You can mail up to $200 worth of goods for personal use; label the package PERSONAL USE and attach a list of its contents and their retail value. If the package contains your used personal belongings, mark it AMERICAN GOODS RETURNED to avoid paying duties. You may send up to $100 worth of goods as a gift; mark the package UNSOLICITED GIFT. Mailed items do not affect your duty-free allowance on your return.

To avoid paying duty on foreign-made high-ticket items you already own and will take on your trip, register them with Customs before you leave the country. Consider filing a Certificate of Registration for laptops, cameras, watches, and other digi-

tal devices identified with serial nu or other permanent markings; you ... keep the certificate for other trips. Otherwise, bring a sales receipt or insurance form to show that you owned the item before you left the United States.

🛈 **U.S. Bureau of Customs and Border Protection** ✉ for inquiries and equipment registration, 1300 Pennsylvania Ave. NW, Washington, DC 20229 ☎ 877/287-8667, 202/354-1000 ⊕ www.customs. gov ✉ for complaints, Customer Satisfaction Unit, 1300 Pennsylvania Ave. NW, Room 5.5D, Washington, DC 20229.

DISABILITIES & ACCESSIBILITY

Hamilton, the Dockyard, and St. George's have sidewalks with sloping ramps (though not on every street corner), but sidewalks are not prevalent elsewhere on the island. Businesses are not required by law to provide access for people with disabilities, but most try to follow the guidelines of the Americans with Disabilities Act (ADA).

If you plan to bring a guide dog to Bermuda, you must **obtain a permit in advance.** Application forms are available from all Bermuda Department of Tourism offices. Once your application is approved, the Department of Agriculture and Fisheries will send an import permit to the traveler; the permit must accompany the dog at the time of arrival. The Bermuda Chapter of the Society for the Advancement of Travel for the Handicapped produces information sheets for travelers with disabilities. You can also get this information at any Bermuda Department of Tourism office.

🛈 **Local Resources** Bermuda Chapter of the **Society for the Advancement of Travel for the Handicapped (SATH)** ✉ 347 5th Ave., Suite 610, New York, NY 10016 ☎ 212/447-7284. **Bermuda Physically Handicapped Association (BPHA)** ✉ Base Gate, 1 South Side, St. David's Island, DD 03 ⌂ Box HM 8, Hamilton, HM AX ☎ 441/293-5035, 441/293-8148 after 5 PM ⌂ 441/293-5036 ⊕ www.bermudaonline.org/BPHA.htm.

LODGING

The most accessible lodgings are the large resorts, such as Elbow Beach and the Fairmont resorts.

RESERVATIONS

When discussing accessibility with an operator or reservations agent, **ask hard questions.** Are there any stairs, inside *or* out? Are there grab bars next to the toilet *and* in the shower/tub? How wide is the doorway to the room? To the bathroom? For the most extensive facilities meeting the latest legal specifications, **opt for newer accommodations.** If you reserve through a toll-free number, consider also calling the hotel's local number to confirm the information from the central reservations office. Get confirmation in writing when you can.

SIGHTS & ATTRACTIONS

Hamilton is hilly and difficult to navigate for people with physical disabilities. City Hall and the Bermuda National Gallery are the city's most wheelchair-friendly sights. The Bermuda Aquarium, Museum & Zoo in Flatts Village between Hamilton and St. George's is also easily accessible for the disabled. St. George's and the Dockyard have cobblestone walks, but are otherwise wheelchair friendly. Horseshoe Beach is the easiest to visit in a wheelchair; taxis can drive up right to the sand. Most beaches have ramps and restrooms that accommodate people with disabilities.

TRANSPORTATION

Public buses in Bermuda are not equipped for wheelchairs. However, the Bermuda Physically Handicapped Association (BPHA) has volunteer-operated buses with hydraulic lifts. Make arrangements in advance.

🚩 Complaints **Aviation Consumer Protection Division** (⇨ Air Travel) for airline-related problems. **Departmental Office of Civil Rights** ⊠ for general inquiries, U.S. Department of Transportation, S-30, 400 7th St. SW, Room 10215, Washington, DC 20590 ☎ 202/366-4648 🖷 202/366-9371 ⊕ www.dot.gov/ost/docr/index.htm. **Disability Rights Section** ⊠ NYAV, U.S. Department of Justice, Civil Rights Division, 950 Pennsylvania Ave. NW, Washington, DC 20530 ☎ ADA information line 202/514-0301, 800/514-0301, 202/514-0383 TTY, 800/514-0383 TTY ⊕ www.ada.gov. **U.S. Department of Transportation Hotline** ☎ for disability-related air-travel problems, 800/778-4838 or 800/455-9880 TTY.

TRAVEL AGENCIES

In the United States, the Americans with Disabilities Act requires that travel firms serve the needs of all travelers. Some agencies specialize in working with people with disabilities.

🚩 Travelers with Mobility Problems **Access Adventures/B. Roberts Travel** ⊠ 206 Chestnut Ridge Rd., Scottsville, NY 14624 ☎ 585/889-9096 ⊕ www.brobertstravel.com ✑ dltravel@prodigy.net, run by a former physical-rehabilitation counselor. **CareVacations** ⊠ No. 5, 5110-50 Ave., Leduc, Alberta, Canada, T9E 6V4 ☎ 780/986-6404 or 877/478-7827 🖷 780/986-8332 ⊕ www.carevacations.com, for group tours and cruise vacations. **Flying Wheels Travel** ⊠ 143 W. Bridge St., Box 382, Owatonna, MN 55060 ☎ 507/451-5005 🖷 507/451-1685 ⊕ www.flyingwheelstravel.com.

DISCOUNTS & DEALS

Be a smart shopper and **compare all your options** before making decisions. A plane ticket bought with a promotional coupon from travel clubs, coupon books, and direct-mail offers or purchased on the Internet may not be cheaper than the least expensive fare from a discount-ticket agency. And always keep in mind that what you get is just as important as what you save.

DISCOUNT RESERVATIONS

To save money, **look into discount reservations services** with Web sites and toll-free numbers, which use their buying power to get a better price on hotels, airline tickets (⇨ Air Travel). When booking a room, always **call the hotel's local toll-free number** (if one is available) rather than the central reservations number—you'll often get a better price. Always ask about special packages or corporate rates.

When shopping for the best deal on hotels, **look for guaranteed exchange rates,** which protect you against a falling dollar. With your rate locked in, you won't pay more, even if the price goes up in the local currency.

🚩 Airline Tickets 🚩 Hotel Rooms **Accommodations Express** ☎ 800/444-7666 or 800/277-1064 ⊕ www.accommodationsexpress.com. **Turbotrip.com** ☎ 800/473-7829 ⊕ www.turbotrip.com.

PACKAGE DEALS

Don't confuse packages and guided tours. When you buy a package, you travel on your own, just as though you had planned the trip yourself. In cities, ask the local visitor's bureau about hotel packages that include tickets to major museum exhibits or other special events.

ECOTOURISM

Bermudians are, on the whole, extremely proud of their island and fairly fanatical about protecting its natural beauty. Still, the concept of ecotourism has yet to find a firm footing. Although the government has been extremely successful in such endeavors as limiting cruise-ship traffic, banning rental cars, and protecting the offshore-reef environment, the typical Bermuda vacation still consists of days by the pool or beach, a few rounds of golf or some water sports, shopping, and (for the adventurous) zipping around from sight to sight on a moped.

ELECTRICITY

Local electrical current is the same as in the United States and Canada: 110 volt, 60 cycle AC. All appliances that can be used in North America can be used in Bermuda without adapters. Winter storms bring occasional power outages.

EMERGENCIES

🔲 Doctors & Dentists Referral **Government Health Clinic** ✉ 67 Victoria St., Hamilton ☎ 441/236-0224 🖷 441/292-7627.

🔲 Emergencies **Air/Sea Rescue** ☎ 441/297-1010 🖷 441/297-1530 ⊕ www.rccbermuda.bm ✐ info@rccbermuda.bm. **Police, fire, ambulance** ☎ 911.

🔲 Hospitals **King Edward VII Memorial Hospital** ✉ 7 Point Finger Rd., outside Hamilton near the Botanical Gardens ☎ 441/236-2345 🖷 441/236-3691.

🔲 Pharmacies **Clarendon Pharmacy** ✉ Clarendon Bldg., Bermudiana Rd., Hamilton ☎ 441/295-9137. **Collector's Hill Apothecary** ✉ South Shore Rd. and Collector's Hill, Smith's ☎ 441/236-9878. **Hamilton Pharmacy** ✉ Parliament St., Hamilton ☎ 441/295-7004 or 441/292-7986. **Paget Pharmacy** ✉ Rural Hill Plaza, Middle Rd., Paget ☎ 441/236-2681. **Phoenix Centre** ✉ 3 Reid St., Hamilton ☎ 441/295-3838 or 441/295-0698. **Robertson's Drug Store** ✉ York St. and Customs House Sq.

☎ 441/297-1736. **White's Pharmacy** Rd., Warwick ☎ 441/238-1050. **Woodbou. Chemist** ✉ Gorham Rd., on outskirts of Hamilton Pembroke ☎ 441/295-1073 or 441/295-2663.

ETIQUETTE & BEHAVIOR

Bermudians tend to be quite formal in attire as well as in personal interactions. Casual dress, including bathing suits, is acceptable at hotels and resorts, but locals seldom venture into Hamilton in anything less than long shorts and sports shirts for men, and slacks-and-blouse combinations or dresses for women. Some restaurants and clubs, particularly those connected to hotels, request that men wear jackets, and more formal establishments require ties during dinner, but there are plenty of places in Hamilton and beyond where you can dress casually and dine well.

In downtown Hamilton, the classic Bermuda shorts are often worn by banking and insurance executives, but the outfit always includes high black socks, dress shoes, and jacket and tie. When it comes to dress, **err on the formal side.** It is an offense in Bermuda to appear in public without a shirt, even for joggers. This rule may seem arcane, but most Bermudians appreciate this decorum. This also holds true for the beach—thong bathing suits and topless sunbathing are not acceptable.

Courtesy is the rule when locals interact among themselves. In business and social gatherings **use the more formal Mr. and Ms. instead of first names,** at least until a friendship has been established, which sometimes takes just a few minutes. Always greet bus drivers with a friendly "Good morning" or "Good afternoon" when you board public buses. This is an island custom, and it's nice to see each passenger offer a smile and sincere greeting when boarding and exiting the bus. In general, respect and appreciation are shown quite liberally to public servants in Bermuda. Although one underlying reason may be the fact that the residents of this small island seem to know one another, and personal greetings on the streets are commonplace, it also seems that a genuinely upbeat and friendly attitude is part of the national character.

GAY & LESBIAN TRAVEL

Bermuda remains socially conservative in many respects, so same-sex couples may encounter some initial uncomfortable moments. However, discriminating against anyone based on sexual orientation is against the law. The Web site www.gaybermuda.com offers information on what to do and where to go.

📌 **Gay- & Lesbian-Friendly Travel Agencies** Different Roads Travel ✉ 1017 N. LaCienega Blvd., Suite308, West Hollywood, CA 90069 ☎ 310/289-6000 or 800/429-8747 (Ext. 14 for both) 🖷 310/855-0323 ✍ lgernert@tzell.com. **Kennedy Travel** ✉ 130 W. 42nd St., Suite 401, New York, NY 10036 ☎ 800/237-7433 or 212/840-8659 🖷 212/730-2269 ⊕ www.kennedytravel.com. **Now, Voyager** ✉ 4406 18th St., San Francisco, CA 94114 ☎ 415/626-1169 or 800/255-6951 🖷 415/626-8626 ⊕ www.nowvoyager.com. **Skylink Travel and Tour** ✉ 1455 N. Dutton Ave., Suite A, Santa Rosa, CA 95401 ☎ 707/546-9888 or 800/225-5759 🖷 707/636-0951; serving lesbian travelers.

HEALTH

Sunburn and sunstroke are legitimate concerns if you're traveling to Bermuda in summer. On hot, sunny days, **wear a hat, a beach cover-up, and lots of sunblock.** These are essential for a day on a boat or at the beach. Be sure to take the same kind of precautions on overcast summer days—some of the worst cases of sunburn happen on cloudy afternoons when sunblock seems unnecessary. Drink plenty of water and, above all, **limit the amount of time you spend in the sun** until you become acclimated.

The Portuguese man-of-war occasionally visits Bermuda's waters, so **be alert when swimming,** especially in summer or whenever the water is particularly warm. This creature is recognizable by a purple, balloonlike float sack of perhaps 8 inches in diameter, below which dangle 20- to 60-inch tentacles armed with powerful stinging cells. Contact with the stinging cells causes immediate and severe pain. Seek medical attention immediately: a serious sting can send a person into shock. In the meantime—or if getting to a doctor will take a while—treat the affected area liberally with vinegar. Ammonia is also an effective antidote to the sting. Although usually encountered in the water, Portuguese men-of-war may also wash up on shore. If you spot one on the sand, steer clear, as the sting is just as dangerous out of the water.

DIVERS' ALERT

Do not fly within 24 hours of scuba diving.

MEDICAL PLANS

No one plans to get sick while traveling, but it happens, so **consider signing up with a medical-assistance company.** Members get doctor referrals, emergency evacuation or repatriation, hot lines for medical consultation, cash for emergencies, and other assistance.

📌 **Medical-Assistance Companies** International SOS Assistance ⊕ www.internationalsos.com ✉ 8 Neshaminy Interplex, Suite 207, Trevose, PA 19053 ☎ 215/245-4707 or 800/523-6586 🖷 215/244-9617 ✉ Landmark House, Hammersmith Bridge Rd., 6th fl., London, W6 9DP ☎ 20/8762-8008 🖷 20/8748-7744 ✉ 12 Chemin Riantbosson, 1217 Meyrin 1, Geneva, Switzerland ☎ 22/785-6464 🖷 22/785-6424 ✉ 331 N. Bridge Rd., 17-00, Odeon Towers, Singapore 188720 ☎ 6338-7800 🖷 6338-7611.

HOLIDAYS

On Sunday and national public holidays, all shops, businesses, and many restaurants in Bermuda close. Buses and ferries run on limited schedules. Most entertainment venues, sights, and sports outfitters remain open. When holidays fall on a Saturday, government and commercial offices close the following Monday, but restaurants and shops remain open.

Bermuda celebrates a two-day public holiday for Emancipation Day/Somers Day and Cup Match in late July, when the whole island comes to a standstill for the annual cricket match between the East and West ends of Bermuda. National public holidays are New Year's Day, Good Friday, Bermuda Day (late May), Queen's Birthday (mid-June), Labour Day (early September), Remembrance Day (early November), Christmas and Boxing Day (Dec. 26).

INSURANCE

The most useful travel-insurance plan is a comprehensive policy that includes coverage for trip cancellation and interruption, default, trip delay, and medical expenses (with a waiver for preexisting conditions).

Without insurance you'll lose all or most of your money if you cancel your trip, regardless of the reason. Default insurance covers you if your tour operator, airline, or cruise line goes out of business. Trip-delay covers expenses that arise because of bad weather or mechanical delays. Study the fine print when comparing policies.

If you're traveling internationally, a key component of travel insurance is coverage for medical bills incurred if you get sick on the road. Such expenses aren't generally covered by Medicare or private policies. U.K. residents can buy a travel-insurance policy valid for most vacations taken during the year in which it's purchased (but check preexisting-condition coverage). British and Australian citizens need extra medical coverage when traveling overseas.

Always **buy travel policies directly from the insurance company**; if you buy them from a cruise line, airline, or tour operator that goes out of business you probably won't be covered for the agency or operator's default, a major risk. Before making any purchase, **review your existing health and home-owner's policies** to find what they cover away from home.

⚡ Travel Insurers In the U.S.: **Access America** ✉ 6600 W. Broad St., Richmond, VA 23230 ☎ 800/284-8300 🖷 804/673-1491 or 800/346-9265 ⊕ www.accessamerica.com. **Travel Guard International** ✉ 1145 Clark St., Stevens Point, WI 54481 ☎ 715/345-0505 or 800/826-1300 🖷 800/955-8785 ⊕ www.travelguard.com.

⚡ In the U.K.: **Association of British Insurers** ✉ 51 Gresham St., London EC2V 7HQ ☎ 020/7600-3333 🖷 020/7696-8999 ⊕ www.abi.org.uk. In Canada: **RBC Insurance** ✉ 6880 Financial Dr., Mississauga, Ontario L5N 7Y5 ☎ 800/565-3129 🖷 905/813-4704 ⊕ www.rbcinsurance.com. In Australia: Insurance Council of Australia Insurance Enquiries and Complaints, Level 3, 56 Pitt St., Sydney, NSW 2000 ☎ 1300/363683 or 02/9251-4456 🖷 02/9251-4453 ⊕ www.iecltd.com.au. In New Zealand: **Insurance Council of New Zealand** ✉ Level 7, 111-115 Customhouse Quay, Box 474, Wellington ☎ 04/472-5230 🖷 04/473-3011 ⊕ www.icnz.org.nz.

MAIL & SHIPPING

Allow 7 to 10 days for mail from Bermuda to reach the United States, Canada, or the United Kingdom, and about two weeks to arrive in Australia or New Zealand.

OVERNIGHT SERVICES

Overnight courier service is available to or from the continental United States through several companies. Service between Bermuda and Canada takes one or two business days, depending on the part of Canada; between Bermuda and the United Kingdom, generally two business days; and between Bermuda and Australia or New Zealand, usually three.

In Bermuda, rates include pickup from anywhere on the island. Prices for a document up to the first pound range from $26 to $37 to the United States, from $30 to $38 to Canada, and from $35 to $42 to the United Kingdom, Australia, or New Zealand. For the fastest delivery, your pickup request must be made before about 10 AM. Note that pickups (and drop-off locations) are limited on Saturday, and there is no service on Sunday. Packages sent to Bermuda may take a day longer than documents.

⚡ Major Services DHL Worldwide Express ☎ 441/295-3300. Federal Express ☎ 441/295-3854. International Bonded Couriers ☎ 441/295-2467. Mailboxes Unlimited Ltd. ☎ 441/292-6563. Sprint International Express ☎ 441/296-7866. United Parcel Service ☎ 441/295-2467.

POSTAL RATES

Airmail postcards and letters for the first 10 grams to the United States and Canada cost 70¢. Postcards to the United Kingdom cost 80¢, letters 85¢ for the first 10 grams. Postcards to Australia and New Zealand cost 90¢, letters 95¢ for the first 10 grams.

RECEIVING MAIL

If you have no address in Bermuda, you can have mail sent care of General Delivery, General Post Office, Hamilton HM GD, Bermuda.

SHIPPING PARCELS

Through Parcel Post at Bermuda's post office, you can send packages via either International Data Express (which takes 2 to 4 business days to the United States and Canada and 3 to 7 days to the United Kingdom, Australia, and New Zealand) or Air Parcel Post (which takes 7 to 10 business days to the United States, Canada, and the United Kingdom, or two weeks to Australia and New Zealand).

For the first 500 grams, International Data Express rates are $25 to the United States and Canada, $30 to the United Kingdom, and $38 to Australia or New Zealand. Air Parcel Post rates run $7.65 for the first 500 grams to the United States, $9.10 to Canada, $11.95 to the United Kingdom, and $14.95 to Australia or New Zealand.

Most of Bermuda's largest stores offer shipping of purchases. Some may ask you either to buy insurance or to sign a waiver absolving them of any responsibility for potential loss or damage.

▲ Post Office International Data Express ☎ 441/297-7802. **Parcel Post** ☎ 441/297-7875.

MEDIA

E-MAIL

If your hotel doesn't hook you up, you may send and receive e-mail for about $12 per hour at a few places around the island, two of which are also restaurants.

▲ E-mail Services Freeport Seafood Restaurant ✉ 1 Freeport Rd., Dockyard, Sandys ☎ 441/234-1692 ✎ freeport@ibl.bm. **Internet Lane** ✉ 22 Reid St., Hamilton ☎ 441/296-9972 ⊕ www.internetlane.net. **M. R. Onions Restaurant and Bar** ✉ Par-La-Ville Rd., Hamilton ☎ 441/292-5012 🖷 441/292-3122 ⊕ www.bermuda.bm/onions. **Twice Told Tales Bookstore** ✉ Parliament St., near Reid St., Hamilton ☎ 441/296-1995 🖷 441/296-6339 ✎ pfowkes@ibl.bm.

NEWSPAPERS & MAGAZINES

The *Royal Gazette,* Bermuda's only daily newspaper, is considered the paper of record. Established in 1828, it is published Monday through Saturday and offers a comprehensive mix of international hard news along with sports, business, and features. Its weekly sister paper, the *Mid-Ocean News,* is more business oriented and features in-depth articles on island politics. Published twice a week, the *Bermuda Sun* also focuses on local politics, trends, events, and entertainment.

Appearing monthly in the *Royal Gazette, RG* magazine is a high-quality glossy, with topical features. *The Bermudian,* the island's oldest monthly, is another glossy, highlighting the people, food, homes, gardens, and heritage of Bermuda.

Six times per year, both the *Bottom Line* and *Bermudian Business* publish business news, commentary, and analysis.

RADIO & TELEVISION

Dial Mix 106 (106.1 FM) for calypso, reggae, and soca, plus R & B, adult contemporary, local jazz, and European classical. For country music, listen to 1450 Country (1450 AM), which also has a midday call-in talk show covering hot local issues. Z2 (1340 AM) surrounds its talk shows with Billboard Top 100 and country-and-western tunes. You can hear more Top 100 rock, R & B, hip-hop, and reggae on Power 95 (94.9 FM). Gospel, easy listening, and religious talk are the sounds on ZFB 1230 AM. Conservative programs can be found on the Bible Broadcasting Network (1280 AM), an all-Christian radio station. Hott 107.5 (FM) is Bermuda's newest and trendiest radio station and specializes in hip-hop, R & B, and gospel. The Government Emergency Broadcast Station (1610 AM) is used in case of a storm.

In addition to a slew of cable television stations (mainly from the United States), Bermudian sets can be tuned in to ZBM ("Zed BM"), the CBS affiliate, on TV channel 9 or cable 3; ZFB ("Zed FB"), the ABC affiliate, on TV channel 7 or cable 2; and VSB, the NBC affiliate, on TV channel 11 or cable 4. Along with the nightly news, local programming, which is interspersed with the networks' offerings, might include a cooking show, a cricket or football (soccer) match, or a program on health awareness. Fresh TV provides exclusively local programming, mostly music- or religion-oriented, on TV channel 3.

MONEY MATTERS

Since Bermuda imports everything from cars to cardigans, prices are very high. At an upscale restaurant, for example, you're bound to pay as much for a meal as you would in New York, London, or Paris: on average, $60 to $80 per person, $120 with drinks and wine. There are other options, of course; the island is full of coffee shops, where you can eat hamburgers and french fries with locals for about $9. The same meal at a restaurant costs about $15.

A cup of coffee costs between $1.50 and $3; a mixed drink from $5 to $8; a bottle of beer from $3 to $6; and a can of soda about $1.50. A 15-minute cab ride will set you back about $25 including tip. A 36-exposure roll of 35mm 100 ASA print film costs $7 to $8. A pack of cigarettes costs between $5 and $7. Prices throughout this guide are given for adults. Substantially reduced fees are almost always available for children, students, and senior citizens. For information on taxes, see Taxes.

ATMS

ATMs are found all over Bermuda, in shops, arcades, supermarkets, the airport, and two of the island's banks. Both the **Bank of Bermuda** and the **Bank of Butterfield** are affiliated with the Cirrus and Plus networks. Note that both banks' ATMs only accept personal identification numbers (PIN) with 4 digits.

CREDIT CARDS

Most shops and restaurants accept credit and debit cards. Some hotels insist on cash or traveler's checks, so check in advance whether your hotel takes credit cards. The most widely accepted cards are MasterCard, Visa, and American Express. Discover and Diners Club are welcomed to a much lesser degree. Throughout this guide, the following abbreviations are used: AE, American Express; D, Discover; DC, Diners Club; MC, MasterCard; and V, Visa. Most 800 numbers incur a toll when dialing from Bermuda, so you may want to call your company collect.

⏞ **Reporting Lost Cards American Express** ☎ 800/441-0519. **Diners Club** ☎ 800/234-6377. **Discover** ☎ 800/347-2683. **MasterCard** ☎ 800/622-7747. **Visa** ☎ 800/847-2911.

CURRENCY

The Bermudian dollar is on par v U.S. dollar, and the two currencie: used interchangeably. (Other non-Bermudian currency must be converted.) You can use American money anywhere, but change is often given in Bermudian currency. Try to avoid accumulating large amounts of local money, which is difficult to exchange for U.S. dollars in Bermuda and expensive to exchange in the United States.

CURRENCY EXCHANGE

If you need to exchange Canadian dollars, British pounds, or other currencies, for the most favorable rates **change money through banks.** Although ATM transaction fees may be higher abroad than at home, ATM rates are excellent because they're based on wholesale rates offered only by major banks. You won't do as well at exchange booths in airports or rail and bus stations, in hotels, in restaurants, or in stores. To avoid lines at airport exchange booths, get a bit of local currency before you leave home.

⏞ **Exchange Services International Currency Express** ✉ 427 N. Camden Dr., Suite F, Beverly Hills, CA 90210 ☎ 888/278-6628 orders 🖷 310/278-6410 ⊕ www.foreignmoney.com. **Thomas Cook International Money Services** ☎ 800/287-7362 orders and retail locations ⊕ www.us.thomascook.com.

TRAVELER'S CHECKS

Traveler's checks are widely accepted throughout Bermuda. Lost or stolen, they can usually be replaced within 24 hours. To ensure a speedy refund, buy your own traveler's checks. Don't let someone else pay for them, as irregularities like this can cause delays. The person who bought the checks should make the call to request a refund.

Some hotels take personal checks by prior arrangement (a letter from your bank is sometimes requested).

MOPED & SCOOTER TRAVEL

Because car rentals are not allowed in Bermuda, you might decide to get around by moped or scooter. Bermudians routinely use the words "moped" and "scooter" interchangeably, even though they are different. You must pedal to start a moped, and it carries only one person. A scooter, on the other hand, which starts when you put the key in the ignition, is more powerful and holds one or two passengers.

Think twice before renting a moped, as accidents occur frequently and are occasionally fatal. The best ways to avoid mishaps are to drive defensively, obey the speed limit, remember to **stay on the left-hand side of the road**—especially at traffic circles—and avoid riding in the rain and at night.

Helmets are required by law. Mopeds and scooters can be rented from cycle liveries by the hour, the day, or the week. Liveries will show first-time riders how to operate the vehicles. Rates vary, so it is worth calling several liveries to see what they charge. Single-seat scooter rentals cost from $35 to $53 per day or from $136 to $181 per week. Some liveries tack a mandatory $20 insurance-and-repair charge on top of the bill, while others include the cost of insurance, breakdown service, pickup and delivery, and a tank of gas in the quoted price. A $20 deposit may also be charged for the lock, key, and helmet. You must be at least 16 and have a valid driver's license to rent. Major hotels have their own cycle liveries, and all hotels and guest houses will make rental arrangements. Gas for cycles runs from $3 to $4 per liter, but you can cover a great deal of ground on the full tank that comes with the wheels.

ROAD CONDITIONS

Roads are narrow, winding, and full of blind curves. Whether driving cars or scooters, Bermudians tend to be quite cautious around less-experienced visiting riders, but crowded city streets make accidents all the more common. Local rush hours are Monday through Friday, from 7:30 AM to 9 AM and from 4 PM to 5:30 PM. Road are often bumpy, and they may be slippery under a morning mist or rainfall. Street lamps are few and far between outside of the cities, so be especially careful driving at night.

RULES OF THE ROAD

The speed limit is 35 kph (22 mph), except in the World Heritage Site of St. George's, where it is a mere 25 kph (about 15 mph). The limits, however, are not very well enforced, and the actual driving speed in Bermuda hovers around 50 kph (30 mph). Police seldom target tourists for parking offenses or other driving infractions. Bermuda's seat-belt law does not apply to taxis or buses. Drunk driving is a serious problem in Bermuda, despite stiff penalties. The blood-alcohol limit is 0.08. The courts will impose a $1,000 fine for a driving-while-intoxicated infraction, and also take the driver off the road for about one year. **⑦ Rental Companies Eve's Cycle Livery** ✉ Middle Rd., Paget ☎ 441/236-6247. **Oleander Cycles** ✉ Valley Rd., Paget ☎ 441/236-5235 ✉ Gorham Rd., Hamilton ☎ 441/295-0919 ✉ Middle Rd., Southampton ☎ 441/234-0629 ✉ Dockyard, Sandys ☎ 441/234-2764. **Wheels Cycles** ✉ 117 Front St., Hamilton ☎ 441/292-2245.

PACKING

Bermudians dress more formally than most Americans. **Leave your cutoffs, short shorts, and halter tops at home.** In the evening, many restaurants and hotel dining rooms require men to wear a jacket and tie and women to dress comparably, so bring a few dressy outfits. Some hotels have begun setting aside one or two nights a week for "smart casual" attire, when jacket-and-tie restrictions are loosened. In this case, women should be fine with slacks or a skirt and a dressy blouse or sweater. Bermudian men often wear Bermuda shorts (and proper kneesocks) with a jacket and tie.

During the cooler months, bring lightweight woolens or cottons that you can wear in layers to accommodate vagaries of the weather. A lightweight jacket is always a good idea. Regardless of the season, **pack a swimsuit, a beach-wear cover-up, sunscreen, and sunglasses,** as well as a raincoat (umbrellas are typically provided by hotels). Comfortable walking shoes are a must. If you plan to play tennis, be aware that many courts require proper whites and that tennis balls in

Bermuda are extremely expensive. Bring your own tennis balls if possible.

In your carry-on luggage, **pack an extra pair of eyeglasses or contact lenses and enough of any medication** you take to last a few days longer than the entire trip. You may also ask your doctor to write a spare prescription using the drug's generic name, as brand names may vary from country to country. In luggage to be checked, **never pack prescription drugs, valuables, or undeveloped film.** And don't forget to carry with you the addresses of offices that handle refunds of lost traveler's checks. Check *Fodor's How to Pack* (available at online retailers and bookstores everywhere) for more tips.

To avoid customs and security delays, carry medications in their original packaging. Don't pack any sharp objects in your carry-on luggage, including knives of any size or material, scissors, and corkscrews, or anything else that might arouse suspicion.

To avoid having your checked luggage chosen for hand inspection, don't cram bags full. The U.S. Transportation Security Administration suggests packing shoes on top and placing personal items you don't want touched in clear plastic bags.

CHECKING LUGGAGE

In Bermuda you board and deplane via a staircase. Let this be your guide when deciding how much to carry on.

You're allowed to carry aboard one bag and one personal article, such as a purse or a laptop computer. Make sure what you carry on fits under your seat or in the overhead bin. Get to the gate early, so you can board as soon as possible, before the overhead bins fill up.

Baggage allowances vary by carrier, destination, and ticket class. On international flights, you're usually allowed to check two bags weighing up to 70 pounds (32 kilograms) each, although a few airlines allow checked bags of up to 88 pounds (40 kilograms) in first class. Some international carriers don't allow more than 66 pounds (30 kilograms) per bag in business class and 44 pounds (20 kilograms) in

economy. On domestic flights, the limit is usually 50 to 70 pounds (23 to 32 kilograms) per bag. In general, carry-on bags shouldn't exceed 40 pounds (18 kilograms). Most airlines won't accept bags that weigh more than 100 pounds (45 kilograms) on domestic or international flights. Check baggage restrictions with your carrier before you pack.

Airline liability for baggage is limited to $2,500 per person on flights within the United States. On international flights it amounts to $9.07 per pound or $20 per kilogram for checked baggage (roughly $640 per 70-pound bag), with a maximum of $634.90 per piece, and $400 per passenger for unchecked baggage. You can buy additional coverage at check-in for about $10 per $1,000 of coverage, but it often excludes a rather extensive list of items, shown on your airline ticket.

Before departure, **itemize your bags' contents** and their worth, and label the bags with your name, address, and phone number. (If you use your home address, cover it so potential thieves can't see it readily.) Include a label inside each bag and **pack a copy of your itinerary.** At check-in, **make sure each bag is correctly tagged** with the destination airport's three-letter code. Because some checked bags will be opened for hand inspection, the U.S. Transportation Security Administration recommends that you leave luggage unlocked or use the plastic locks offered at check-in. TSA screeners place an inspection notice inside searched bags, which are re-sealed with a special lock.

If your bag has been searched and contents are missing or damaged, file a claim with the TSA Consumer Response Center as soon as possible. If your bags arrive damaged or fail to arrive at all, file a written report with the airline before leaving the airport.

Bermuda-bound airlines commonly accept golf club bags in lieu of a piece of luggage, but there are fairly stringent guidelines governing the maximum amount of equipment that can be transported without an excess baggage fee. The general rule of

...overed bag containing a
...of 14 clubs, 12 balls, and 1 pair
...

...omplaints **U.S. Transportation Security Ad-
...inistration Consumer Response Center** ☎ 866/
289-9673 ⊕ www.tsa.gov.

PASSPORTS & VISAS
When traveling internationally, **carry your passport,** even if you don't need one (it's always the best form of ID), and **make two photocopies of the data page** (one for someone at home and another for you, carried separately from your passport). If you lose your passport, promptly call the nearest embassy or consulate and the local police.

U.S. passport applications for children under age 14 require consent from both parents or legal guardians; both parents must appear together to sign the application. If only one parent appears, he or she must submit a written statement from the other parent authorizing passport issuance for the child. A parent with sole authority must present evidence of it when applying; acceptable documentation includes the child's certified birth certificate listing only the applying parent, a court order specifically permitting this parent's travel with the child, or a death certificate for the nonapplying parent. Application forms and instructions are available on the Web site of the U.S. State Department's Bureau of Consular Affairs (⊕ www.travel.state.gov).

ENTERING BERMUDA
Citizens of the United States or Canada should **bring a passport to ensure quick passage through immigration and customs.** You do not need a passport to enter Bermuda if you plan to stay less than six months, but you must have onward or return tickets and proof of identity, such as an original or certified copy of your birth certificate with raised seal, or another certificate of citizenship (Naturalization Certificate, Alien Registration Card, or Reentry Permit), and a photo ID. However this is about to change, and it will soon be a requirement for U.S. visitors to carry a passport in Bermuda, at all times.

Citizens of the United Kingdom and other countries must have a valid passport to enter Bermuda.

PASSPORT OFFICES
The best time to apply for a passport or to renew is in fall and winter. Before any trip, check your passport's expiration date, and, if necessary, renew it as soon as possible.
🚩 Australian Citizens **Passports Australia** ☎ 131-232 ⊕ www.passports.gov.au.
🚩 Canadian Citizens **Passport Office** ✉ to mail in applications: 200 Promenade du Portage, Hull, Québec J8X 4B7 ☎ 819/994-3500, 800/567-6868, 866/255-7655 TTY ⊕ www.ppt.gc.ca.
🚩 New Zealand Citizens **New Zealand Passports Office** ☎ 0800/22-5050 or 04/474-8100 ⊕ www.passports.govt.nz.
🚩 U.K. Citizens **U.K. Passport Service** ☎ 0870/521-0410 ⊕ www.passport.gov.uk.
🚩 U.S. Citizens **National Passport Information Center** ☎ 900/225-5674 or 900/225-7778 TTY (calls are 55¢ per minute for automated service or $1.50 per minute for operator service), 888/362-8668 or 888/498-3648 TTY (calls are $5.50 each) ⊕ www.travel.state.gov.

SAFETY
Don't wear a money belt or a waist pack, both of which peg you as a tourist. Distribute your cash and any valuables (including your credit cards and passport) between a deep front pocket, an inside jacket or vest pocket, and a hidden money pouch. Do not reach for the money pouch once you're in public.

Bermuda is a small, affluent country and as a consequence has a low crime rate. Serious crimes against visitors—or anyone, for that matter—are rare. Still, **exercise the usual precautions with wallets, purses, cameras,** and other valuables, particularly at the beach. If you are driving a moped, always travel with your purse or bag concealed inside the seat. Always lock your moped or pedal bike, and store valuables in your room or hotel safe. Although an ocean breeze through a screen door is wonderful, **close and lock your hotel room's glass patio door** while you're sleeping or out of your room. After sunset, stick to the main streets in Hamilton and St. George's. Court Street in Hamilton is a little rough even in the daytime. Use common-sense precautions as you would in any unfamiliar environment, and be alert while walking at night.

SENIOR-CITIZEN TRAVEL
Special rates are available for seniors traveling on Bermuda's public ferries and buses, and some pharmacies and department stores offer discount days for seniors.

To qualify for age-related discounts, **mention your senior-citizen status up front** when booking hotel reservations (not when checking out) and before you're seated in restaurants (not when paying the bill). Be sure to have identification on hand.

🔁 Educational Programs **Elderhostel** ✉ 11 Ave. de Lafayette, Boston, MA 02111-1746 ☎ 877/426-8056, 978/323-4141 international callers, 877/426-2167 TTY 🖷 877/426-2166 ⊕ www.elderhostel.org.

STUDENTS IN BERMUDA
There are no youth hostels, YMCAs, or YWCAs on the island. During Bermuda Spring Break Sports Week, however, special student rates are offered at some hotels and guest houses, restaurants, pubs, and nightclubs.

🔁 IDs & Services **STA Travel** ✉ 10 Downing St., New York, NY 10014 ☎ 212/627-3111, 800/777-0112 24-hr service center 🖷 212/627-3387 ⊕ www.sta.com. **Travel Cuts** ✉ 187 College St., Toronto, Ontario M5T 1P7, Canada ☎ 800/592-2887 in the U.S., 416/979-2406 or 866/246-9762 in Canada 🖷 416/979-8167 ⊕ www.travelcuts.com.

TAXES
Hotels add a 7.25% government tax to the bill, and most add a 10% service charge or a per-diem dollar equivalent in lieu of tips. Other extra charges sometimes include a 5% "energy surcharge" (at small guest houses) and a 15% service charge (at most restaurants).

A $29 airport-departure tax and a $4.25 airport-security fee are built into the price of your ticket, whereas cruise lines collect $60 in advance for each passenger.

TAXIS
Taxis are the fastest and easiest way to get around the island—and also the most costly. Four-seater taxis charge $5.35 for the first mile and $2 for each subsequent

mile. Between midnight and 6, Sunday and holidays, a 25% added to the fare. There is a 2... for each piece of luggage stored in the trunk or on the roof. Taxi drivers accept only American or Bermudian cash, but not bills larger than $50, and they expect a 15% tip. You can phone for taxi pickup, but you may wait awhile while the cab navigates Bermuda's heavy traffic. Don't hesitate to hail a taxi on the street.

For a personalized taxi tour of the island, the minimum duration is three hours, at $30 per hour for one to four people and $42 an hour for five or six, excluding tip.

🔁 Cab Companies **The Bermuda Industrial Union Taxi Co-op** ☎ 441/292-4476. **Island Wide Taxi Services** ☎ 441/292-5600. **Bermuda Taxi Radio Cabs** ☎ 441/295-4141, 441/295-0041 to arrange taxi tours. **Sandys Taxi Service** ☎ 441/234-2344.

TELEPHONES
Telephone service in Bermuda is organized and efficient, though service may be interrupted during storms.

AREA & COUNTRY CODES
The country code for Bermuda is 441. When dialing a Bermuda number from the United States or Canada, simply dial 1 + 441 + local number. You do not need to dial the international access code (011). The country code is 1 for the United States and Canada, 61 for Australia, 64 for New Zealand, and 44 for the United Kingdom.

CELL PHONES
Most travelers can use their own cell phones in Bermuda, though you should check with your provider to be sure. Cell-phone rentals are available from stores in Hamilton and St. George's.

🔁 Rentals **All Talk** ✉ 27 York St., St. George's ☎ 441/297-3151. **BermudaCellRentals.com** ✉ The Armoury Bldg., 37 Reid St., Hamilton ☎ 441/232-2355. **Internet Lane** ✉ The Walkway, 22 Reid St., Hamilton ☎ 441/296-9972.

DIRECTORY & OPERATOR ASSISTANCE
When in Bermuda, call 411 for local phone numbers. To reach directory assistance from outside the country, call 441/555-1212.

ERNATIONAL CALLS

Most hotels impose a surcharge for long-distance calls, even those made collect or with a phone card or credit card. Many toll-free 800 or 888 numbers in the United States aren't honored in Bermuda. Consider buying a prepaid local phone card rather than using your own calling card. In many small guest houses and apartments the phone in your room is a private line from which you can make only collect, credit-card, or local calls. Some small hotels have a telephone room or kiosk where you can make long-distance calls.

You'll find specially marked AT&T USADirect phones at the airport, the cruise-ship dock in Hamilton, and King's Square and Ordnance Island in St. George's. You can also make international calls with a calling card from the main post office. You can make prepaid international calls from the Cable & Wireless Office, which also has international telex, cable, and fax services Monday through Saturday from 9 to 5.

To call the United States, Canada, and most Caribbean countries, simply dial 1 (or 0 if you need an operator's assistance), then the area code and the number. For all other countries, dial 011 (or 0 for an operator), the country code, the area code, and the number. Using an operator for an overseas call is more expensive than dialing direct. For calls to the United States, rates are highest from 8 AM to 6 PM and discounted from 6 PM to 8 AM and on weekends.

�07 **To Obtain Access Codes** AT&T USADirect ☎ 800/872-2881. MCI Call USA ☎ 800/888-8000 or 800/888-8888. Sprint Express ☎ 800/623-0877.
�07 **International Calls** Main post office ⊠ Church and Parliament Sts., Hamilton ☎ 441/295-5151. **Cable & Wireless Office** ⊠ 20 Church St., opposite City Hall, Hamilton ☎ 441/297-7000

LOCAL CALLS

To make a local call, simply dial the seven-digit number.

LONG-DISTANCE SERVICES

AT&T, MCI, and Sprint access codes make calling long-distance relatively convenient, but you may find the local access number blocked in many hotel rooms.

First ask the hotel operator to connect you. If the hotel operator balks, ask for an international operator, or dial the international operator yourself. One way to improve your odds of getting connected to your long-distance carrier is to travel with more than one company's calling card (a hotel may block Sprint, for example, but not MCI). If all else fails, call from a pay phone.

�07 **Access Codes** AT&T Direct ☎ 800/872-2881. MCI WorldPhone ☎ 800/888-8000. Sprint International Access ☎ 800/623-0877.

PHONE CARDS

Buy a prepaid a phone card for long distance calls. They can be used with any touch-tone phone in Bermuda, although they can only be used for calls outside Bermuda. Rates are often significantly lower than dialing direct, but the down side is that some hotels will charge you for making the call to your card's 800 number. Phone cards are available at pharmacies, shops, and restaurants. The phone companies Cable & Wireless, TeleBermuda, and Logic Communications sell prepaid calling cards in denominations of $5 to $50. The cards can be used around the world as well as in Bermuda.

�07 **Phone Card Companies** Cable & Wireless ☎ 441/297-7022. Logic Communications ☎ 441/296-9600. TeleBermuda ☎ 441/296-9000.

PUBLIC PHONES

You'll find pay phones similar to those in the United States on the streets of Hamilton, St. George's, and Somerset as well as at ferry landings, some bus stops, and public beaches. Deposit 20¢ (U.S. or Bermudian) before you dial. Most hotels charge from 20¢ to $1 for local calls.

TIME

Bermuda is in the Atlantic Time Zone. Bermuda observes Daylight Saving Time (from the first Sunday in March to the last Sunday in October), so it's always one hour ahead of U.S. Eastern Standard Time. Thus, for instance, when it is 5 PM in Bermuda, it is 4 PM in New York, 3 PM in Chicago, and 1 PM in Los Angeles. London is four hours, and Sydney 14 hours, ahead of Bermuda.